ACKNOWLEDGMENTS

I'd like to thank a legal secretary with a great sense of humor, Sally Steuterman, and my longtime neighbor, Debbie Fein, for some secretarial books I could never have found. I'd also like to thank a couple of secretaries turned comedians: Anita Wise and Kathleen Garrity; and a former temp turned comic, Barry Steiger. I appreciate the assistance of Mr. Peter ("The Temp") Grossman, Wendi and Chris Hahn, and the support of my wonderful family, which will (by the printing of this book) include my wife, Carol, whose writing credits now include five of the following pages.

This book is dedicated to a possible future secretary, Jennifer Leigh.

Finally, I'd like to salute all the diligent secretaries, ladies and gents, who work for male and female employers (some of whom aren't ladies and gents). We've made a concerted effort, chapter by chapter, throughout the book to include both gender of employers, and both gender of secretaries. We did not bother, however, to distinguish computer genders. In other words, we didn't turn any Wangs, or IBMs upside-down to check.

695
150

HOW TO QUALIFY FOR THE THANKLESS POSITION AS A GLAMOROUS, UNDERPAID SECRETARY!

Do you measure up to the secretarial challenge? This quiz will let you know whether you've got what it takes to make it on nearly no-money-a-week (and all the ball-point pens you can "borrow"):

A Rolodex is:
a) A circular file for phone numbers
b) A desk on rollerskates
c) An expensive wristwatch

A letter marked confidential means:
a) The letter contains information that requires protection
b) Your boss is having an affair

Wite-Out:
a) Eliminates typing mistakes
b) Is a funky new nail polish
c) Occurs during electrical storms

When the copy machine breaks down, the best thing to do is:
a) Call the repairman
b) Kick it, then go home
c) Turn it into a planter

THE UNOFFICIAL SECRETARY'S HANDBOOK

RICHARD MINTZER is the author of several books. He conducts humor-writing seminars in Manhattan.

THE UNOFFICIAL SECRETARY'S HANDBOOK

by
Richard Mintzer

PRODUCED BY
ULTRA COMMUNICATIONS, INC.

A PLUME BOOK
NEW AMERICAN LIBRARY
NEW YORK AND SCARBOROUGH, ONTARIO

NAL BOOKS ARE AVAILABLE AT QUANTITY DISCOUNTS WHEN USED TO PROMOTE PRODUCTS OR SERVICES. FOR INFORMATION PLEASE WRITE TO PREMIUM MARKETING DIVISION, NEW AMERICAN LIBRARY, 1633 BROADWAY, NEW YORK, NEW YORK 10019.

Illustrations by Rosemary Slader

PLUME TRADEMARK REG. U.S. PAT. OFF. AND FOREIGN COUNTRIES
REGISTERED TRADEMARK—MARCA REGISTRADA
HECHO EN CHICAGO, U.S.A.

SIGNET, SIGNET CLASSIC, MENTOR, ONYX, PLUME, MERIDIAN and NAL BOOKS are published *in the United States* by NAL PENGUIN INC., 1633 Broadway, New York, New York 10019, *in Canada* by The New American Library of Canada Limited, 81 Mack Avenue, Scarborough, Ontario M1L 1M8

Library of Congress Cataloging-in-Publication Data

Mintzer, Richard.
The unofficial secretary's handbook.

"Produced by Ultra Communications"
1. Office practice—Anecdotes. 2. Secretaries—Anecdotes. 3. Office practice—Humor. 4. Secretaries—Humor. I. Netter, Susan. II. Title.
HF5547.5.M564 1988 651.3'741'0207 88-12499
ISBN 0-452-26156-2

First Printing, October, 1988

1 2 3 4 5 6 7 8 9

PRINTED IN THE UNITED STATES OF AMERICA

Contents

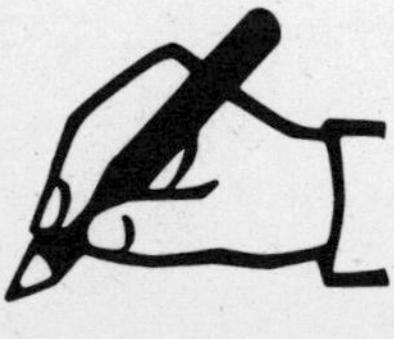

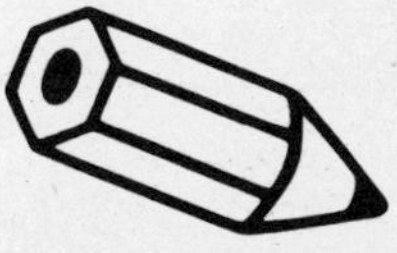

PART 1

Getting Started

Introduction

Dear Secretary,

You're part nurse, part teacher, part baby-sitter, part genius, and part saint. Your skills must include not only shorthand and typing, but patience, loyalty, tact, diplomacy, second-guessing, method acting, and mind-reading. Plus the kind of spontaneity that would make you a perfect contestant for *The Newlywed Game*.

Naturally, we're talking about the bulwark of the business world, without whom every office, service, and industry would cease to function and crumble to disarray—the secretary. More often than not, you're the power behind the throne and the brains of the outfit, the one who really understands the action and can make a rational decision and just scrawl the appropriate initials or signature. After all, you don't want to interrupt during an important luncheon meeting or afternoon brainstorm session; it's just as important for you to keep him protected and away from the madding office crowd as it is to keep him "tuned in." What he doesn't know won't hurt him.

So, here's to secretaries everywhere. This book is for you and about you and your particular environment. We hope it tickles your funnybone, touches your heart, and most of all, makes others—especially your boss—appreciate you for the gem you are. So, when you're through with it, make sure you place it on top of his In Box!

Sincerely yours,
The Company

COULD YOU MAKE IT AS A SECRETARY?
A Quiz

1. **Wite-Out:**
   (A) Eliminates typing mistakes.
   (B) Is a funky new type of nail polish.
   (C) Occurs during an electrical storm.

2. **Your actual typing speed is:**
   (A) 45 to 60 words per minute.
   (B) 60 to 80 words per minute.
   (C) 40 to 50 mistakes per minute.

3. **A Rolodex is:**
   (A) A circular flip-over file for phone numbers.
   (B) A desk on roller skates.
   (C) An expensive wristwatch.

4. **When you're asked to "take a letter," you:**
   (A) Use shorthand to take down your boss's verbal ramblings.
   (B) Remove a letter key from your typewriter.
   (C) Swipe a sealed envelope from the outgoing mail.

5. **Often you fantasize about:**
   (A) Moving up the corporate ladder.
   (B) Pushing your boss out a third-story window.
   (C) Xeroxing your breasts and slipping a copy into that cute young executive's In Box.

6. **When filing, you'd put "The Nabisco Corp." folder under:**
   (A) *N* for Nabisco.
   (B) *T* for The.
   (C) *C* for crackers.

7. **You have lunch plans with a friend, and your boss asks you to go to the bank for him. You would:**
   (A) Cancel your lunch plans.
   (B) Take an extra hour for lunch to accomplish both tasks, plus buy a new sweater.
   (C) Explain to him that the banks are always closed on Spiro Agnew's birthday.

8. **To put "CC" on a memo or letter means:**
   (A) Send copies of the memo to other, specified people.
   (B) The memo is closed-captioned.
   (C) The memo is for Chevy Chase.

9. **When the copy machine breaks down, the best thing to do is:**
   (A) Call the service representative.
   (B) Kick it, scream at it, and then go home.
   (C) Turn it into a planter and order a newer, more sophisticated model.

10. **You discover a letter addressed to your boss buried beneath the mess on your desk. You open the envelope to find an invitation to a dinner tomorrow night that should have been RSVP'd a week ago. You would:**
   (A) Give your boss the invitation and apologize.
   (B) Call in the RSVP, explaining that your boss is too ill to attend.
   (C) Rip up the invite and throw it in the wastebasket, where you would have "filed" it anyway.

The Six-Year-Old Secretary

How to Spot the Early Signs and Symbols

Is there such a thing as a "born secretary"? Could nature be so cruel, or, in the case of her future bosses, so kind? Check out the following early warning signs often exhibited by young secretaries-to-be.

1. She alphabetizes the noodles in her alphabet soup.
2. She asked for a Xerox machine for Xmas.
3. The first time she answered the phone, she asked the caller to, "Please hold while I find Mommy."
4. For her birthday she wanted you to "order in from McDonald's."

5. She learned to type before she could walk.
6. She brings coffee to her daddy with the morning mail—without being asked!
7. She always picks flowers from the garden for her mom's birthday and tells her they're from her dad.
8. She wants to play "office" instead of "house" or "doctor."
9. She tries to file her coloring books according to subject matter.
10. She began to "take minutes" in kindergarten.

The Top Ten Reasons for Becoming a Secretary

1. You were born to type.
2. You enjoy the power of being able to put top executives on hold for hours or even days.
3. *Nine to Five* was your all-time favorite movie.
4. You love to doodle and thought by learning shorthand you could get paid for it.
5. You aspire to move up the corporate ladder because the phrase "expense account" has always sounded good to you.
6. You have an overwhelming urge to spend forty hours a week, or more, in an office building, and you love waiting for elevators.
7. You dream of introducing new and exotic blends of coffee to the business world.
8. You love running up enormous phone bills and not having to pay for them.
9. Xeroxing is your favorite means of artistic self-expression.
10. You need staplers, pens, pencils, legal pads, and other office supplies in your home, and don't want to buy them.

Secretaries of the Rich and Famous

The following quotes are what their secretaries had to say about the following well-known bosses.

President Lincoln: "I wish I had forgotten to pick up those theater tickets on my lunch hour."

Dr. Ruth Westheimer: "The hardest thing was taking her messages and trying not to blush at the four-letter words."

George Steinbrenner: "I was always packing and unpacking. He must have fired and rehired me eight or ten times."

Pee Wee Herman: "Do you have any idea how difficult it is to take steno in crayon?"

Johnny Carson: "Alimony Check Sending Day always means overtime."

Jeane Dixon: "She not only knew when the mail came in, but she knew what was inside before I had a chance to open it."

Bella Abzug: "At lunch she lets me shop for as long as I want to, provided I buy her a hat."

Vanna White: "When she says take a letter, she means it literally."

Dom DeLuise: "Sometimes lunch was a business trip."

Marcel Marceau: "He had the only video Dictaphone."

Pablo Picasso: "His memos were impossible to decipher, but they brought me a fortune when I sold them to a local museum."

Lawrence Welk: "Every letter started the same way: 'And a one and a two.' "

Geraldo Rivera: "I distinctly remember telling him . . . Al Capone's vault is probably empty, don't waste your time! But did he listen?"

Richard Nixon (Rosemary Woods): "I meant to hit fast forward and hit erase instead. So what's all the big commotion about?"

Patrick Duffy: "How come *I* never get to find him in the shower?"

Julie Andrews: "Supercalifraji . . . what?"

Santa Claus: "After he checks the list twice, who do you think checks it the third time?"

GREAT DATES IN SECRETARIAL HISTORY

2,000,000 B.C.	Caveman gets tired of etching pictures on cave walls and asks a young female to do it for him in exchange for peanuts.
1,000,000 B.C.	Eve decides to try out her Apple no matter what Adam says.
1350 B.C.	First shorthand symbols found on Egyptian stone tablet, later translated as a memo from King Tutankhamen to his "female scribe" or secretary, asking her to buy a birthday present for his wife.
900 B.C.	Moses admits that the Ten Commandments were taken down not by him but by his "secretarium."
1492	Christopher Columbus's secretary plans his travel itinerary and includes a stop in the "New World."
1819	The Florida Purchase is made by a secretary on a long lunch-hour shopping spree.
1911	Katharine Gibbs sells her jewelry to open the first secretarial school.
1912	Katharine Gibbs buys back her jewelry with the money earned from her secretarial school.
1924	A secretary in Illinois tries to invent Wite-Out by mixing nail polish with baking powder.
1933	Secretary Jane Dorment puts Mr. P. J. Cummings on hold. It is the first time anyone has ever been put on hold, and a confused Mr. Cummings remains motionless at his desk for four days.
1948	The first secretarial convention is held. At the opening meeting, 2,200 sets of minutes are taken.
1958	A secretary sets a never-to-be-broken world's record by typing for five hours while keeping a hoola hoop spinning. She then calls in sick for the next three days, complaining of PMS (Perpetual Motion Syndrome).

1962	Three Motown secretaries form the Supremes. The one named Diana can't type, but nobody cares.
1963	A Massachusetts secretary attempts to create Wite-Out by mixing shredded paper and cream cheese.
1968	At an antiwar rally, two secretaries are arrested for burning their bras. A third, less intelligent, radical junior secretary suffers minor burns to her chest.
1972	Comic actress Carol Burnett creates the lackadaisical character Mrs. Wiggins, a secretary with as much get up and go as a dead parrot.
1973	Rosemary Woods learns how to use a tape recorder.
1983	The well-known Mayflower Madam fires her secretary for refusing to "entertain" male clients during an extended lunch hour.
1984	The United States Secretarial Team wins two gold medals at the Olympic Games. It is the first time that Secretarial Skills are included as an event.
1987	World's record for document shredding is set by a Washington, D.C., secretary/boss team.
1987	Former church secretary poses nude in men's magazine, explaining that it pays better.

Secretarial School

The Course, the Fun, and Dress Codes

Yes, there is a place where secretaries are mass-produced, and it's called secretarial school. Here you will learn the essential skills needed to become a first-rate secretary. You'll learn typing, steno, how to send appropriate correspondence, and how to look right and dress properly while always remaining poised and polite. The skills will remain with you throughout your business career(s). The dress code will stay with you as far as the job interviews, and perhaps the first few weeks on the job (unless you become a legal secretary). The idea of being completely subservient, and rarely ever using your own ingenuity, will go out the window the day of graduation.

Most secretarial schools were set up when bosses were men, and secretaries were property. The attitudes have changed in the latter half of the twentieth century. The modern secretary is often out to ingest as much knowledge as possible in hopes of climbing the corporate ladder. Other secretaries may be quite content in their role as caretaker to a semi-helpless boss. But, whatever the scenario, the role of the secretary is no longer played by a damsel in distress.

So, if you are heading for secretarial school, you may want to skip the course in curtsying, but you'll benefit greatly by taking one in word processing, along with the classics, typing, steno, etc. In short, you may wish to ingest the skills, and regurgitate the attitudes.

The Courses

BUSINESS COMMUNICATIONS 1

The ability to communicate clearly is essential to the business community. In this course you'll learn never to say what you are really thinking. You'll learn proper techniques in office gossip, back stabbing, disclosing secret information, how to lie with a straight face, and how to serve up b.s. with a smile.

ACCOUNTING 101

In this course you will learn the basics of accounting and gain insight into how one writes off weekends in Bermuda and Club Med vacations as business trips. You'll learn how to fidget with digits and balance your personal checking account.

INTRODUCTION TO TYPING

Here you will be formally introduced to the newest member of your family, your typewriter. You will learn the keyboard, the proper fingers to use, the best way to cheat when nobody's looking, and how not to break a nail.

INTRODUCTION TO GREGG SHORTHAND

You will learn the proper methods of doodling and scribbling at rapid speed in order to accurately transcribe a speaker's utterances, no matter how meaningless and inane. Course meets twelve hours a week, or until your fingers are too cramped to move.

AMERICAN HISTORY—PART 1

Learn who transcribed the Gettysburg Address, who proofread the Constitution, who made Ben Franklin coffee, who Xeroxed copies of Betsy Ross's flag, and who typed up Dear John reply letters for our soldiers in World War I.

BUSINESS CORRESPONDENCE

Learn to compose business letters, amusing memos, letters of resignation, and how to fit a self-addressed stamped envelope into an envelope of equal size without folding it. Become familiar with the procedure needed to send personal mail through the office to avoid having to pay postage.

BUSINESS LAW
You'll become familiar with creative embezzlement, insider trading, bogus tax deductions, and other things your boss will hope that you know nothing about. Learn the term "sexual harassment" and how much you can earn from a good lawsuit.

ECONOMICS
Become familiar with money, and how little of it you are actually earning. Learn how to make money grow, how to manage it, print it, beg, borrow, and steal it. You'll become familiar with foreign rates of exchange in the event that your boss tries to pay you in yen, pesos, or poultry.

GREGG SHORTHAND 2
You'll learn to write faster than the speed of sound. Special techniques include psychic transcription, which will have you taking down what your boss will say just prior to his saying it.

AMERICAN HISTORY—PART 2
Starting with the Second World War, you'll learn who dialed and got through to Castro for JFK during the Cuban Missile Crisis, and how "clever" secretaries saved their bosses' necks by whiting out names from McCarthy's blacklist. You'll study Rosemary Woods and her tape player, Fawn Hall and her shredder, and Jessica Hahn and her "off the books" income.

ADVANCED BUSINESS COMMUNICATIONS
Learn to read written communications more precisely, as well as facial expressions, hand gestures, intentional sighs, grunts, groans, howling, Morse Code, tribal drum beating, foot stamping, obscene phone calls, or any other method by which your future boss may choose to communicate.

PROFESSIONAL DEVELOPMENT
Here you'll learn how to give service with a smile, how to wear your hair with an administrative flair, how to dress for success, and numerous other trite and pointless clichés.

CONVENTION PLANNING
In this course you'll become familiar with the essentials of a successful convention. Learn to register two dozen Mr. and Mrs. Smiths, where the nearest bars are, where to get an appropriate stripper (male or female, depending on the convention), where to get a cake big enough for them to jump out of, and how much in petty cash is available for bail money.

ADVANCED TYPING
Learn to move your fingers so fast that your eyes can no longer follow them. Become familiar

with switching margins with your elbows and changing ribbons with your teeth, to keep you from ever having to stop typing or look away from your copy.

OFFICE INFORMATION SYSTEMS

Because technology has revolutionized the business world, you will be made familiar with word processors, multidimensional phone systems, microwave ovens, laser pencil sharpeners, digital staple removers, vibrating rubber fingers, and other supermodern devices designed to speed up efficiency and break down frequently.

GREGG SHORTHAND 3

Learn the deep dark secret mystique of Gregg Shorthand. You'll discover the true answer to what secretary-ism is all about. In short, you'll learn who Gregg is!

Dress Codes

As you enter secretarial school you will be enrolling in an institution that will try to duplicate a business environment as closely as possible. You'll be expected to dress as you would on a job interview. We at the Secretarial Academy expect our students to look professional at all times.

HAIR

Clean, well-groomed hair is a must. Your hair should not frame your face, fall in your eyes, or resemble Tina Turner's. You should have easy-to-manage hair—preferably short—that needs as little attention as possible. We recommend the "Tennis Ball" cut, where your hair is too short to do anything with, and you're embarrassed to be seen in public.

BLOUSES

Simply cut, solid-color blouses are suggested. Frilly blouses give the impression that you're a push-over, while see-through blouses give the impression that you enjoy being pushed over.

SKIRTS

These are not advised for male secretaries. For ladies, straight-cut, pleated, solid, or tweed skirts are recommended. Green, navy, or any other dull color that gives a hint of being a parochial school graduate, or social-scene drop-out, are ideal for the secretarial school student. Slit skirts may prolong job interviews an extra hour or so, while miniskirts will help you get hired, but not for the skills you trained at. A tight skirt may create an enticing image, but you'll have a hard time (and look silly) standing while trying to type.

BLAZERS AND JACKETS

Blazers can add a lot to your look. A red blazer will give you that tour guide/crossing guard look, while a blue blazer will help you attain a new level of respect, since you'll resemble a law enforcement officer. Dark colors reflect a businesslike, no-nonsense attitude. White blazers or jackets, on the other hand, prompt ice cream orders, startle borderline schizophrenics, and don't take well to spilled coffee. Cowhide or fringed jackets are acceptable only if you're working for Ben Cartwright or J. R. Ewing.

DRESSES

Anything that's slightly behind the height of fashion is acceptable in secretarial school. Low-cut necklines are considered hazardous during filing, or while leaning over the copier. A tailored wrap dress is always nice, provided you don't have a habit of getting yourself caught on typewriter carriages while walking through the office.

SWEATERS

Over a blouse, a sweater can enhance your outfit. Under a blouse, a sweater would look ridiculous. Worn by itself, a sweater can also look nice, provided it fits without accentuating any parts of your anatomy.

Finally, T-shirts, tank tops, and halters should only be worn on summer days when your boss is out of town.

PART 2

Getting Hired

SECRETARIAL CLASSIFIED ADS
Reading Between the Lines

Secretarial help-wanted ads are likely to promise almost anything in their attempt to lure you into taking the job. Here are some typical ads from the Sunday paper, followed by a translation of what each ad really means:

WHAT THE AD SAID	WHAT IT REALLY MEANT
Motion picture mogul seeks sharp sec'y-asst. with interest in show biz. Must have exc. skills and be flexible.	Your knees better be flexible so you can kneel down and worship this show biz has-been who's also a dirty old man.
Your creative style and flair are needed in the adv. dept. of mags that help shape the fashion world. Good oppt. Art courses/training helpful.	We need a novice who's well-dressed and fashionable, with original ideas for us to steal while we pay her peanuts.
Get involved! Act as right hand to director of city planning program in large downtown company.	Work for a lazy civil service employee, who'll have you doing absolutely everything as his right hand while taking graft with his left.
Two cream puff positions with terrific bosses. Hurry and call Robin!	Two male travel agents promised Robin a week in the Bahamas if she'd "fix them up."

Political rights organization seeks secretary for wide range of duties. 16K to start, plus 4 wks vacation. Exp. not req. We will train.	Terrorist group needs someone to type up inflammatory propaganda and deliver mail bombs at incredibly low pay. We give long vacations in case you have to leave the country suddenly.
Exec. Secy.—Rewarding spot for a well-rounded patriotic Miss who's discreet and can handle top-secret assignments. Must be good with paperwork. Luxury office bldg. Washington, D.C., location. 20K—commissions possible.	In other words, we're looking for a well-stacked babe to pose as a sec'y and double as an escort for visiting heads of foreign states. She has to know when to keep her mouth open or shut and how to shred paper.
Top financial service firm seeks articulate, well-educated, exp. executive secretary comfortable in the corporate atmosphere. Type 70, Steno 90. Excellent benefits, profit-sharing.	Ideal place to have absolutely no fun whatsoever. Gray or blue suits (and ties), the need to refer to everyone on a last-name basis, and positively no sense of humor required.
Financial executive needs top-notch secretary with knowledge of acquisitions and purchasing.	Executive needs someone who knows how to purchase jewelry and clothing for his wife.
Import/export company seeks experienced bilingual secretary to handle busy phones. Flexible hours.	Company seeking someone who can lie proficiently on behalf of the boss in various languages, and do so at 4 A.M. if necessary.
First-rate secretary sought! Established, mature, senior V.P. is looking for a secretary with top skills. Duties also include scheduling appointments, handling financial affairs, and attending meetings. Other skills a plus.	Aging V.P. needs someone to schedule his proctologist appointments, go to the bank for him, do his tax returns, and keep him awake at meetings. CPR training a plus.
Summer's coming! Top Ten ad agency gets out at noon on Fridays! Openings in all areas, creative, sales, marketing, etc. Room for advancement. Type 55.	If you have no desire to take your job seriously, and want to get the most out of your weekends, then this job is for you. Possible advancement to coming in late on Mondays!

Employment Agencies

So Many Applicants, So Few Jobs, So Little Money

If you should find yourself unemployed, with no "good leads" and no relatives who strongly favor nepotism, you may consider going to an employment agency. These so-called job finders are ideal if you're searching for a low-paying job in the worst part of town.

Secretaries are in demand, so agencies will usually try to accommodate you. You must beware of their accommodations however, as some agencies will send you for jobs that simply aren't for you. Many a secretary has had to say things like, "I do love animals, but secretary to a snake charmer isn't quite right for me. No, it's not the money . . ." Don't be persuaded to take a job at an accounting firm if your background includes three years of secretarial work for a ballet company. The phrase "Don't worry, you'll catch on" is highly overused by employment agency counselors.

Upon entering an employment agency you must prepare yourself to be drilled, grilled, rated, interrogated, debated, and asked one hell of a lot of unnecessary questions. This will accompany the joyous task of filling out the application.

The standard application asks for personal information, such as name, address, phone number, birthday, social security number, shoe size, the date you lost your virginity, and other necessary facts. Next you will be required to list and describe every job you've ever had, tell how much it paid, and explain why you left. Answering the last part is often difficult, since explaining that your boss made you sick to your stomach is hard to squeeze into the allotted space. Consider these alternative answers: boss dropped dead, company went down the toilet, some bitch stole my job, couldn't work with ex-lover, or my parents objected, might be shorter ways of explaining why you left a particular position.

Education is an important part of job applications. You should have some education, but not too much. After all, you don't want your counselor to know you're smarter than she is. Next to the box where you list the name of the school is generally a box for you to indicate your major. This is understandable for listing your college major, and acceptable for high school. The question that arises is; What are you honestly supposed to put in that box when you get down to grammar school? Perhaps you can list that you majored in coloring neatly between the lines.

A biggie on any secretarial application is the space where you fill in your skills. Here you should include; typing, steno, coffee making, filing, answering a telephone, watering plants, and karate. Below that they'll want to know what machines you know how to operate. Here you should include everything from the Xerox machine to a hair dryer.

After completing the application and waiting a sufficient amount of time comes the fun part of the day, your typing test. It is at this point you realize that your ability to translate Shakespearean plays into Latin is totally useless (as is everything you just wrote on the application) if you don't move those fingers fast enough. To illustrate this point, we refer to a Yale student who completed a master's thesis on animal behavior in 1978. The student went to five of New York's leading agencies and sent a trained chimpanzee in to take the typing test. Four of the five agencies found employment for the animal solely based on his typing speed. The fifth didn't find a job for the animal, explaining that they don't base everything on a single typing test. They stated that "the chimp made a terrible cup of coffee."

A typing test is generally given in a small room, where you are instructed to type a two-page letter, including charts, graphs, a diagram, and a list of Arabic symbols. You work on a machine that has more mileage than a '68 Chevy and you have two minutes to complete the test. Afterward, you are graded with one point given for correct words and a lit match touched to a part of your body for every incorrect word.

Yes, employment agencies are fun places, run by people whose greatest pleasure is seeing you squirm, and whose favorite words are "We'll see what we can do for you." Someday, if you're lucky, you'll have your chance to "thank" them.

Interviews: Dos and Don'ts

Here are a few things to remember to do during an interview:

1. Make eye contact. You must make eye contact during the interview, but not with yourself, since a cross-eyed secretary is usually a horrible typist. Blinking a lot might be construed as flirting or a contact lens problem. Staring the interviewer down may not get you the job, but if it does, at least your boss will know who the real boss is.

2. Be confident in your answers to all questions. Forgetting where you went to high school (as Bo Derek did on *The David Letterman Show*) is quite embarrassing. Inverting your 62 WPM typing score to 26 WPM could be more damaging to your future, however. Speak loudly enough so that the interviewer can hear you, but not loudly enough to interrupt dictation taking place down the hall. It is most important to exhibit a sense of pride in your abilities: "Of course I can take shorthand"; "Filing's a breeze"; "I can make coffee with my eyes closed," etc.

3. Be agreeable. If the "Boss to be" says the sky is green, and you want the job, then the sky is green. If the boss says he needs a hard worker, willing to do overtime, then you're just that type of diligent nose-to-the-grindstone type of secretary. If the boss says she wants to give you a private interview at her place, point to that "green" sky and tell her she's going to see stars in it if she thinks you're going to her place.

Even more important, remember *not* to do the following:

1. Don't do your nails.
2. Don't offer to do the interviewer's nails.
3. Don't eat your lunch off the interviewer's desk.
4. Don't take down all of the interviewer's questions in shorthand to try and impress her.
5. Don't wear your Walkman.
6. Don't ask more questions than the interviewer.
7. Don't complain about the office decor or make tasteful suggestions about how they could redecorate.
8. Don't ask to use her phone for a personal call.
9. Don't try to pass yourself off as a Fawn Hall lookalike.
10. Don't play with the interviewer's Wang.
11. Don't hand in five resumes and ask that they select the one they like the best.
12. Don't do your impression of Judy Garland or Lucille Ball, especially if you're a male.

There's No Business Like . . .

Almost every profession employs secretaries at some level. The question is, therefore, what type of company do you want to work for? Here is a list of various types of businesses with their strong and weak points:

ADVERTISING	*Strengths:* Glamorous; free products; shortened hours on Fridays in the summer. *Weakness:* Work for people who'd gladly sell their own grandparents into slavery to get more people to put the right brand of bread on their dining room tables.
PUBLISHING	*Strengths:* Prestigious; learn the business; work with people who know proper grammar. *Weaknesses:* No money, ever! Bosses change weekly.
BANKING	*Strengths:* Learn what CDs, IRAs, and other banking terms really mean, work in a dignified atmosphere; earn respectable money. *Weaknesses:* Bankers are boring; no parties; too many numbers; no good gossip; dull wardrobe.
ENTERTAINMENT	*Strengths:* Glamorous; meet famous people; lots of wild parties; free drugs. *Weaknesses:* Meeting famous people; going to too many wild parties; too many free drugs; can't get ahead without giving it.
POLITICS	*Strengths:* Learn about the workings of the government; overhear great gossip; be a part of national scandals. *Weaknesses:* Work with people you don't trust; become an accessory to all sorts of criminal activities; be under constant surveillance.

LAW	*Strengths:* Good benefits; great dating prospects; long vacations; high pay. *Weaknesses:* Dealing with pompous lawyers; multiple bosses; endless workdays; tedious research.
TEXTILE/ GARMENT INDUSTRIES	*Strengths:* Lots of free time during off season; discounts on furnishings and clothes. *Weaknesses:* Dealing with narcissistic salespeople; don't earn enough to put up with these salespeople.
EDUCATION	*Strengths:* Great hours; long vacations; tons of holidays; great medical benefits. *Weaknesses:* Screaming children; screaming parents; screaming teachers and principals; pre–World War II office equipment; have to fight coworkers for supplies.
ACCOUNTING FIRMS	*Strengths:* Good money; prestigious positions; taxes done correctly (and for free); free financial advice. *Weaknesses:* Dull wardrobe; no office jokes.

PART 3

Friends and Foes

A Secretary by Any Other Name

Technically you may be a secretary, but before long you will find that word is actually an umbrella term that encompasses a number of other job descriptions and functions that you will be expected to perform—usually in the space of one day, if not one hour. Was Sybil, the famed schizophrenic with sixteen personalities, really a secretary? You may think so after you read the following list of alter egos you may be forced to assume during the curse—that is, *course*—of your career . . .

1. Nanny . . . because most bosses are big babies.
2. Handwriting Analyst . . . when you have to transform scribbles into neatly typed letters.
3. Key Keeper . . . for the files—and more importantly for the bathrooms.
4. Waiter . . . specializing in fetching and pouring coffee.
5. Editor . . . to make your boss's letters sound coherent.
6. Proofreader . . . to make your typing look coherent.
7. Audience . . . to your boss's bad jokes.
8. Accountant . . . to figure out exactly how underpaid you are and how overpaid he is.
9. Telephone Operator . . . trying to juggle twelve calls at once.
10. Juggler . . . trying to do twelve things at once.
11. Purchasing Agent . . . buying not only office supplies but gifts for the boss's spouse or mistress, or both.
12. Mind Reader . . . so you

can do all those things your boss forgets to tell you about but expects you to get done.

13. Gardener . . . because your boss doesn't know an aloe from an African violet.
14. Referee . . . to pull co-workers' hands from around your boss's throat.
15. Nurse . . . so you can take care of your boss's aches and pains.
16. Psychologist . . . so you can soothe your neurotic boss's emotional problems.
17. Masseuse . . . so you can massage your boss's ego.
18. Right Fielder . . . to play behind your boss (the first baseman) and back up all his errors—on the company softball team and in the office.
19. Detective . . . to find out where your boss left his reading glasses, his pen, his datebook, his brain, etc.
20. Administrative Assistant . . . for those days when you're in no mood to be any of the above, especially a secretary!

Secretarial Types

They Come in All Sizes, Shapes, and Species

DEDICATED DEBBIE

She's from the "old school," even if she isn't old herself. This gal is not only her boss's best friend and right hand—she's the "power behind the throne" as well. Dedicated Debbie will work almost as hard as Lady Macbeth herself to help her often-incompetent boss to get ahead in the company, for no other reward except that she did her best to make him the best. Other secretaries often hate and fear Dedicated Debbie simply because she is so selfless and efficient. She does things by the book and always performs in top form. She lives for her job and doesn't really understand her coworkers who seem to have "personal lives" outside of the office. Debbie's so good at her job that even the president of whatever company she works for is in awe of her and even a bit fearful. That's because he knows deep down that Dedicated Debbie could do his job much better than he can.

SALLY, THE SOCIAL DIRECTOR

Sally not only knows the birthday of every employee, but their wedding anniversary, their children's birthdays, and the date on which they were initially employed. She spends an inordinate amount of time planning parties, sneaking cakes into the office, ordering flowers, and buying greeting cards to be passed around for all to sign. She has candles in her paper clip box, plastic forks in her filing cabinet, and wrapping paper in her Out Box. A sweet soul who cares about everyone individually, Sally the Social Director not only remembers to ask about coworkers' kids, but their cats, too. And if you're single, divorced, or eligible in any way, Sally will go out of her way to match you—or in most cases mismatch you—with someone she knows or has heard of. Sally seldom finds the time to do any actual secretarial work, but she's such a warm and caring person that her bosses seldom complain. They either do the work themselves or foist it off on some unsuspecting office drone while Social Sally, the queen bee, goes on her merrymaking way.

GRAND OLD GAL FRIDAY

Concerned with everyone's health and welfare, this senior secretary doubles as the office granny. Her desk is equipped with packets of chicken soup, tea bags, cold remedies, and Band-Aids. By the same token, the Grand Old Gal herself is a storehouse of old wives' tales, fabulous folk tales, and awful anecdotes that actually happened to her friends, relatives, neighbors, and herself. She's also an expert on office trivia and can inform any employee about the last nine people who held that particular job. She's the only person in the office who can embarrass your boss by reminiscing about his first day on the job as the office mail boy. As for her own boss, he's a saint on earth. And actually, you have to agree with this assessment, seeing as how he keeps on the Grand Old Gal even though she is completely baffled by the new phone system, not to mention the computer. Always remember to squelch dirty jokes when this Grand Old Gal Friday is within earshot. And if you see her sneaking a shot at her desk, don't ask for any—it's not Bailey's Irish Cream, but Phillips' Milk of Magnesia.

GOSSIPING GAIL

At first glance, this gal looks very efficient because she's always on the phone, either recording information or reporting it. She also types a lot, but too often she's taking down top-secret information about one fellow employee or another, which she can't wait to pass along. On the surface, Gossiping Gail appears to be friendly and outgoing, inviting new and unsuspecting employees to be her confidantes. If you do confide in Gail, the most intimate details of your personal life will soon be broadcast all over the office! She knows who's dating whom, who's mated with whom, and most important, how much everyone makes. Beware, because Gail is helpful, offering to cover for you if you're away from your desk; but by the time you return, she'll have uncovered every smidgen of information your desk has to offer, including fingerprints. Bosses shrewd enough to realize Gossiping Gail's talents often utilize her as an office spy. Others wonder why the CIA hasn't already recruited her.

BORED BARRY

This secretary looks as though he's only had three hours of sleep—in the last week. He doesn't bother to try and conceal his yawns—his reflexes aren't fast enough—and he's been known to fall asleep at his desk even when listening to his Walkman. Coffee has no apparent effect on Barry, even though he sips it all day; in fact, his trips to the men's room and the coffee machine represent the only proof that he is, indeed, alive on any given day. As far as Bored Barry's office skills are concerned, he types fifty words per week and answers the phone after seven rings. He can make an entire day's work out of sharpening pencils and refilling the stapler. Harried bosses find Barry's easygoing, unflappable nature soothing to their frazzled nerves. Even getting screamed at and fired repeatedly doesn't get to him. He just shrugs and then moseys on back to work the next day as if nothing had happened . . .

SUZY THE SEXBOMB

Suzy's main concern is looking her best at all times. She spends her lunch hours getting her hair done, her coffee breaks getting manicures, and half her working day in the ladies' room, fixing her face. No matter what the weather, Suzy wears short skirts, low-cut tops, and a seductive smile. She's very conscientious about her boss's interoffice memos, often adding on cute, suggestive little messages of her own and scenting them with her perfume. Suzy is very dedicated—not only to her boss, but to other males in the company who may be in need of her services. She doesn't mind it a bit when her expert shorthand techniques lead to long hours, and she's been known to take dictation in elevators and cabs.

BOSSES:

From the Sublime to the Slime

See if you can match your boss to one on our list . . .

MR. OR MS. MOODY

A temperamental or moody boss can turn life in the office into a roller-coaster ride. One day everything smells like roses and the next day you're getting stuck by the thorns. You can usually tell by the way your boss says "good morning" what kind of day you're in for. If he looks you straight in the eye and says a clear "good morning" you're in luck. However if your boss looks down and mumbles, be prepared.

Moody bosses are quick-tempered and can be set off faster than a firecracker if you should accidentally light the fuse. Disturbing them for anything less than an oncoming tornado, or simply leaving them out when ordering up a pizza for lunch, could spell disaster. Moody bosses will scream and yell a lot, and foot stamping isn't entirely out of the question. It's unfortunate that you can't play umpire and eject them from the office. During their most pronounced displays of juvenile behavior, your job is to be extremely polite, pop a Valium if possible, and try to remain dignified. This can be difficult if your boss is jumping up and down on the desk screaming, "This copy's too light! I can't read a #@#%$X word!"

The most intriguing thing about temperamental bosses is that when they are in a "good" mood, they will totally downplay their alter ego, or in this case, their other mood. "I guess I was a little upset yesterday," the boss will utter with a sheepish grin, while you sit there recalling the difficulty you had in prying his hands from around the messenger's throat. It is also very important to ask for raises, days off, vacations, or pose any work-related questions while he is in this "good" mood. Getting something in writing and making a copy (for when he tears the original up in a fit of anger) is a good idea. This way you have proof that Mr. Hyde was Dr. Jekyll when he said you could leave early for that doctor's appointment.

Despite the drawbacks of the temperamental boss's bad days, working for this type of boss can be very exciting. From day to day, and sometimes from hour to hour, you never know what to expect. It's almost like working in the middle of a suspense novel.

Below are a few ways you might be able to tell your moody boss's mood in advance:

1. Did he win or lose his bet on Monday night football?
2. Is his spouse away on a business trip? Does he have a standby? Is she out of town too?
3. Does your boss have a meeting scheduled with anyone he has been avoiding for the past six months, such as a tax auditor, bill collector, or district attorney?
4. Did you notice someone else's car in your boss's assigned parking space when you came to work? How bad were the traffic reports? How delayed were the trains and buses?

THE ROUND-THE-CLOCKER

"One, two, three o'clock, four o'clock work, five, six, seven o'clock, eight o'clock work, nine, ten, eleven o'clock, twelve o'clock work, we're gonna work around the clock tonight." If those lyrics have you thinking of your boss, then you're working with a Round-the-Clocker, also known as a Workaholic.

Workaholics don't believe in a nine-to-five workday. They prefer the twenty-four-hour deli style, whereby you always have the opportunity to be working. This boss doesn't understand the concept of a full hour for lunch, and prefers eating over his papers. These papers even accompany this toiling turkey to the restroom. If a call comes in at 8:45 or 5:15, this boss is always ready to take it, as long as it's business related. Along with your never-ending stream of duties, it's your moral obligation, if nothing else, to occasionally remind your workaholic boss that he does have a family by tapping the photos on his desk and commenting on how lovely the children are. You might also choose to remind him of their names.

It's rather useless to ask this kind of boss what he did over the weekend, because it probably had something to do with a new marketing strategy or old paperwork. Inviting the workaholic to company parties is also unnecessary, since he probably will be too busy to attend. Should this type of boss actually show up at a social gathering, you can be sure he will find a quiet corner in which to discuss new policies with a fellow workaholic V.P.

The Round-the-Clocker will indulge a little bit by entering the football pool. But you'll have to find out who won the games, since the boss won't find the time to watch them.

The astounding thing about this overly energetic employer is that he will always find something to do. On the slowest day of the year, perhaps immediately preceding Christmas, the workaholic boss will still be dictating letters and punching up a few numbers on the adding machine. It will finally take several extremely inebriated members of the building maintenance crew to physically remove him from the office in time for Christmas.

A total enigma to this kind of leader are personal phone calls. His idea of a personal call is taking two minutes to call a broker and buy or sell half a dozen stocks. Yes, these nose-to-the-grindstone fanatics have plenty of money. Why shouldn't they, since they spend every waking hour making it and never have time to spend it.

All you can do is remain busy, propose an occasional business idea to show you're on the ball, and pretend you care as much as the boss does. Get very upset when the market drops, and cheer when his new proposal is a hit at the board meeting. As for trying to cure the Round-the-Clocker, forget it. At one time there was a Workaholics Anonymous, but it went out of business since none of its members would ever take the time off to show up at the meetings.

NERVOUS NORMAN (OR NORMA)

To this boss you should only serve decaffeinated coffee, since the real thing will only make matters worse. This boss stands over your shoulder praying as you speak to the Chairman of the Board, and listens closely for any stoppages in typing. The nervous type paces while dictating letters, waiting for visitors, and occasionally while eating lunch. In fact, Nervous Norman's chair is in the best shape of any in the office, since he can't sit still.

The nervous boss has an aching fist from pounding the broken copy machine, sore feet from walking the stairs rather than waiting for the elevator, and fingers that twitch from tapping a pencil on the desk all day. Before you can get the phone up to your ear, your boss will want to know who's calling. What makes matters worse is that when Mr. (or Mrs.) Jitters wants to speak with you, or shout at you, the intercom is simply too difficult to operate.

When taking a letter from this type of boss, you should have a couple of good erasers, a six-pack of Wite-Out, and a reserve notepad handy. This boss will reiterate and rearrange the words faster than in a game of electronic Scrabble. On the Dictaphone you'll find yourself hitting fast forward and rewind more than the play button.

You stand a slight chance of soothing this shaky leader if you can teach him to relax. You could suggest a massage, possibly an Oriental-style massage, which would enable you to walk all over your boss for a change. However, chances are good that the nervous boss tosses and turns a lot when lying down, which would send an Oriental masseuse flying out the window. You can forget teaching Nervous Norman and Norma yoga, as they won't sit still long enough to relax. Perhaps your best bet is slipping a mild tranquilizer into their coffee.

Here are a few ways to spot a nervous boss:

1. Are his or her pencils well chewed?
2. Do guests need a towel to dry their hands after shaking your boss's sweaty palm?
3. Does your boss interrupt his own lunch to call an impromptu meeting to be sure everything is running smoothly?

THE METICULOUS MANIAC

When your boss complains that you put the stamp half an inch closer to the corner of the envelope than you're supposed to, then you know you're dealing with a Meticulous Maniac. This boss cares about every minute detail and will go out of his way to drive you mad. You'll be double- and triple-checking everything you do and still this fanatical supervisor will have you re-retyping the letter because on line five you only left one space after a period and not two.

The meticulous boss keeps plenty of records on who's doing what, when, and where. Your trips to the copy room, washroom, or any other room will be noted. You'll also find yourself doing plenty of filing, since everything is kept in duplicate or triplicate. Your boss will show up at 9 A.M. on the dot, and you'd better be sitting at your desk, ready to work.

A good secretary for this type of maniac should have a background that includes straight As in spelling, punctuation, and grammar, as well as ballet classes, since you'll constantly have to be on your toes.

It is not for you to ask why or how your boss became this way. Reading Freud, Jung, or Joyce Brothers won't help you explain why your boss wants you to answer the phone precisely in the middle of the third ring, or why his trips to the rest rooms are at 10:00, 12:15, and 3:28 daily. Your job is simply to do better than the best humanly possible.

To keep your sanity while working for the Meticulous Maniac, you have three options open to you:

1. Attend "Perfection Training" seminars.
2. Try to work slowly enough to do everything right: three

hours to type a two-paragraph letter, fifteen attempts to make a cup of coffee that would make Brazil proud, do not leave one task until it is carried through to its ultimate completion, etc.

3. You can fight fire with fire and try to drive your meticulous boss crazy. Put his pencils away in the wrong order, with broken points, bend his paper clips slightly, move his blotter a half inch to the right, tell him one of his pants legs is shorter than the other. The sadistic possibilities are endless and may well result in diverting the Meticulous Maniac's attention away from you and *your* mistakes . . . especially when the men in the white coats come for him.

SPEEDY GONZALEZ

Can your boss break the world dictation record of nineteen letters in seven minutes? Does he brag to visitors about your 90 WPM typing speed? Is the office VCR stuck on fast forward?

If the answers to the preceding questions are yes, then you may be working for a speed merchant. These bosses can do their nine-to-five routine in three hours flat and spend the remainder of the day trying to get the rest of the staff to catch up with them. The built-for-speed boss blurts out new ideas from the mouth before his brain has had time to fully formulate them. It's your job always to be prepared and keep a straight face.

This boss believes in churning out work, quantity over quality. Twenty meaningless memos a day far surpass one sensible, well-thought-out letter in this boss's mind. Therefore it's your job to produce! Haste may make waste, but in this case a full wastepaper basket means you've been on a roll.

Instant coffee is never ready fast enough for this swift supervisor. You have to be in early and brewing by 8:58 so that when your boss comes flying out of the elevator, complaining about how long it took to get to the third floor, you'll be ready. Roller skates will help you get from the kitchen to your desk before your fleet-footed leader. The only way to keep up with this type of boss is using the Radar O'Reilly Method of anticipating what the boss will do seconds before he lets fly with it.

Here are a few courses that might help you keep pace with this drag-racing boss:

1. Evelyn Wood's speed reading course.
2. Evelyn Wood's speed writing course.
3. Evelyn Wood's speed eating course.
4. Evelyn Wood's speedy retirement course.

THE SENIOR PARTNER

The senior staffer is often still hanging around because he's suspicious of the junior partners or his wife won't let him retire to hang around the house and drive her crazy all day. Instead, you have the honor of letting him drive *you* crazy.

This boss lives in antiquated fashion, looks at your wardrobe with a bit of disbelief, but never complains about the slit in your skirt. After all, it may be your legs that keep him from retiring.

He is unfamiliar with computers and word processors and will not attempt to learn how to use them (although he pretends to know how). The new telephone system also baffles him, and he doesn't believe in the conference call feature. Instead he'll have you call each party separately to ask them the same question. Sometimes he refers to videos as kinnies (Kinescopes), and other times he's in search of an inkwell for his pen. But all of this adds to his charm.

If you think along the same lines, agree a lot, and practice extreme courtesy, the senior boss will treat you like a grandchild. No, you won't get money every time he sees you, but he'll take your word for things. Pretty soon you'll have not only his trust, but complete control of the office.

Since he does very little actual work, you'll be able to do whatever you want to throughout most of the day provided he believes it has some vital importance to the company. Thus you may find yourself saying things like, "No, I'm not blow-drying my hair. I spilled water on these papers and I'm trying to dry them."

Senior partners won't fire a good secretary very often. Once you've adjusted to their ways they won't want anyone else working in your place. You may even begin to feel a sense of guilt when you take a sick day or leave on your vacation. You should not worry, however, if the senior partner has a large corner office, there's a good chance he owns part of the company.

THE PLAYBOY

Does your boss have six phone lines tied up with female callers named Grace, Shirley, Cindy, Phoebe, Kitten, and Boom-Boom? If this is the case, and you're a female secretary, look out. If you're a male secretary, start following your boss around with a notepad and pencil.

Any woman working for this type of boss is well advised, if she has lunch with the boss, to keep the subject on business, and let him do most of the drinking. If you can introduce him to your six-foot five-inch boyfriend (real or impersonated), you're in good shape. If not, learn karate and destroy the phone book before his very eyes. Once you've built the appropriate office relationship you're safe, unless you actually are interested in Mr. Playboy. In that case, play hard but not impossible to get, and accidentally Wite-Out his little black book to eliminate some of the competition.

In the working relationship, you'll have to guide your boss into the twentieth century, where women are people too. If he calls the new V.P. of marketing Babe, or refers to a visiting overseas executive as that Swiss chick, you may have to explain, through gritted teeth, that these are not the titles either woman has spent the past five years working to achieve.

Keeping a scorecard is also important, so that you don't send Sally to his luncheon appointment with Sue, or flowers to Marcie that were meant for Darcy,. You'll also have to keep track of his incredible lies. Therefore, you may choose to attend a Pathological Liars Anonymous meeting so that you'll be better able to communicate with your Playboy boss.

The Playboy generally has one thing on his mind and an abundance of dirty jokes to help him express it. He will make an occasional remark about your anatomy, in which case it's best to hold up a short pencil and tell him that you're also thinking of his anatomy.

Knowing his social calendar is a plus for any good secretary, because you're in a perfect position to screw it up. Reminding him of this fact will help during salary negotiations.

THE TOP JOCK

Working for this type of boss means being part of the team, and teamwork always comes first. But why were you assigned the position of relief pitcher, always coming in to clean up the mess that the boss started?

The Top Jock isn't necessarily a naturally gifted athlete. An hour of squash at noon usually has him wiped out for the rest of the day. Nonetheless he's in a great mood if he won or at least played well. And don't worry, if your boss gets a hit during one of the company softball games you'll hear a play-by-play-by-play description throughout most of the following day and possibly the remainder of the week.

You must learn not to snicker when you walk in and find your boss putting in his office or should you notice twenty crumpled-up pieces of paper near the garbage can.

This is the kind of boss who takes the events at the company picnic seriously, not to mention his prominently displayed bowling trophies. To the Top Jock, problems with the nine iron far superseded your problems trying to balance the expense account.

The mood of this type of boss will vary, depending on how many touchdowns the Giants, Bears, Lions, or Dolphins scored on Sunday afternoon or Monday night. If you're lucky, his favorite baseball team has a good runproducing lineup, or his favorite hockey team has a great goalie. He'll spend countless hours busily trying to figure out how to end the NFL strike, or who will win the NBA championship. Never fear, if you don't know much about his favorite sport, you'll inevitably find yourself learning through his office jock talk.

Here are a few common sports terms and how they can be applied to an office situation:

1. Double Play: In the office, this baseball term, describing a play in which you get two outs at once, simply means getting rid of two phone callers with one excuse.
2. Fourth End Goal: This football term, describing a last chance to get in to the end zone for a touchdown on a particular series of plays, can be translated in the office to mean a last opportunity to convince the board that his proposal will work before the end of this series of meetings.
3. Pinch Hit: A baseball term whereby one hitter bats in the place of another hitter. In the office it is used to describe your typing up half a dozen extra letters for your ailing coworker.
4. Daily Double: This horse-racing term refers to picking the winning horse in two races prior to the start of the first race. In the office, this is where you and your fellow secretaries bet on which two bosses will come in first on a rainy Monday morning, or which two bimbos in the typing pool will get fired first.

A Miscellany of Bosses

Astronaut: Usually found in the arts, this boss is "spaced," always forgetting times, places, and your name.

Name Dropper: Assumes that your mouth will drop open every time he mentions the names of his top corporate buddies.

Nepotist: Will hire his son, daughter, niece, or nephew, to do any job, even yours, so look out!

Buddy: Thinks you're pals . . . "So, are you still dating that same guy?"

Mr. Martini: You need not worry about typos, because they'll never see clearly enough to notice. Don't light a match nearby after lunch!

Initialist: Prefers to be known as J.B., H.C., Mr. B., or P.P.

Octoboss: Watch out for those extra pairs of hands.

Pseudo Mind Reader: Thinks he knows what everyone is going to do or say before they do or say it. Wrong 83 percent of the time.

The Terminator: You probably won't work for this boss long, as he has a pink slip dispenser in the top drawer. This boss gets a kick out of firing employees and hiring new workers for future "termination."

Wisecracker: Has a sarcastic crack or bad joke ready for any occasion.

Slavedriver: Cracks the whip until 5:01 P.M. You respect this boss whether you like it or not.

Oscar Madison: The well-known slob from Neil Simon's *Odd Couple* often comes to life in the form of a boss who'll have you spending most of your days rummaging through piles, files, and wastepaper baskets searching for lost letters, reports, lunches, etc.

Teacher: Re-explains everything he wants you to do every time he wants you to do it. Explains how to use your stapler, staple remover, etc.

PART 4

Secretarial Compartments

Secretary

A Dictionary Definition

sec·re·tar·y 1. A person employed to handle correspondence, keep files, do clerical work, and create and communicate unmitigated lies for an individual or company. 2. An officer who keeps records of the meetings, stock transfers, illegal transactions, insider trading, and financial blunders of a company or other organization. 3. A hired employee whose sole task is to keep all individuals and organizations from approaching, meeting, or speaking with a corporate executive or antisocial individual. 4. An official presiding over an administrative department of state without letting elected officials know her daily activities or expenditures. 5. A desk with a small bookcase and typewriter on top. (Middle English *secretarie*, from Medieval Latin *secretarius*, confidential officer, secretary, from Latin *secretus*, SECRET, from Pig Latin *ecretaryse*, from Burmese *secrelyer*, keeper of secrets through pathological lying, and from Ancient Greek *secres typrus*, can she type?)

Secretarial Facts—and Fancies

* Secretaries are most often (92 percent) women.

* Secretaries cover for their superiors an average of 2.7 times per day.

* There are more secretaries in the United States than in any other nation in the world. The fewest secretaries are in Iceland, where it's too cold to type and there is no place to go shopping during lunch hour.

* The oldest working secretary is ninety-seven years old. She spends mornings making coffee, taking Geritol breaks, and trying to locate her dentures in the filing cabinet.

* The world's heaviest secretary weighs 412 pounds. Her name is Brenda, and the elevator in her office building says "Capacity: Brenda." She eats lunch at her desk with a knife and forklift, and types twenty-three words per bite.

* The most coffee made by one secretary in one week, for one boss, was sixty-seven cups. The boss completed a forty-hour workweek in twenty-three hours, and spent the rest of the time jogging back and forth between Minneapolis and St. Paul.

* The wealthiest secretary in the world is Howard Hughes's former secretary, who is now worth over seven million dollars. Her only regret was having never met the reclusive Mr. Hughes personally. She continues to work as a secretary for, as she puts it, "The medical benefits."

* The most secretaries in one immediate family are eight members of the Reese family. This includes the mother, six daughters, and one secretarial son. Despite their requests for raises, their boss, Mr. Reese, feels that they are earning enough. He may, however, consider giving them a little of the extra money he is saving, having recently fired Grandma Reese.

* The most secretaries ever to fit in an elevator was seventeen (all female). This occurred in 1973, at Universal Studios. The one man in the elevator at the time was Burt Reynolds.

The Private Secretary

The private secretary plays numerous roles, ranging from surrogate wife to financial manager. As opposed to handling the affairs of a company, your job is to handle the affairs of an individual. An important question private secretaries must ask themselves is how private they want this relationship to become. Many a torrid love affair has begun with a private secretary being asked to pick up satin sheets for her boss or to prepare the boss a home-cooked meal (breakfast).

One step short of the "very private" secretary is the "private pal" interactions. Often a female-female or male-male relationship, this is where the boss confides in the secretary to the point where he/she could start writing the boss's diary. The problems arise when your role surpasses that of a psychologist, clergyman, or counselor, and you realize that your boss is trying to turn you into her clone. You might want to draw the line short of attending family functions.

Private secretaries perform a plethora of personal chores, which include everything from buying Christmas gifts for the boss's family to balancing his checkbook. You may well find yourself controlling the family pursestrings—to the point of being asked whether they can afford a new car this year. "Awkward" might be a euphemism as to how you feel when the boss's wife calls you up for mortgage money the same afternoon when you have to write out a check for his mistress's rent.

To be a good private secretary, you must begin to think in the same manner as your boss. Many will assume that they no longer need bother with memory at all as long as you're there. Knowing what your boss would do or say in any given situation is very important. If your boss is a Republican, you may suddenly have to rethink your own political views, at least during working hours. You may also have to suspend your moral and ethical values . . . if you have any left.

Being a private secretary may not be a nine-to-five job, but this can work both ways. You may well be awakened in the middle of the night by your boss calling from London or Paris to remind you of ten million loose ends you have to take care of, including a birthday present for her favorite niece.

On the other hand, you may find yourself in control of unlimited car services and charge accounts, with your boss encouraging you to use them for your own convenience, both on and off the job. One fortunate secretary found herself in her boss's villa in Rome with a maid and a butler at her disposal. Other secretaries have received their own cars, chances to travel all around the country, and choice theater tickets on the night the boss's son-in-law had strep throat. A good boss will try hard to keep a good private secretary happy . . . because a happy private secretary will keep a boss's secrets private, too.

The Legal Secretary

If you want to be up to your briefs in lawsuits and leases, you should consider becoming a legal secretary. Besides being able to write in legal jargon, you must be able to understand the legal vocabulary and put up with those who expound upon it, such as lawyers and judges.

Being familiar with legal matters is helpful, but hopefully not from your firsthand experience with the police. Slapping a fresh junior attorney is secondary to knowing how to slap a subpoena on a witness.

To your advantage, you can get free legal advice, learn how to read your lease, and threaten to sue anyone who crosses your path the wrong way. You'll be a hit at family gatherings helping your uncle organize his affluent estate while working your way into the will, and helping your sister pad her belly and slap a paternity suit on her ex-boyfriend. As a legal secretary you'll even have the rare opportunity to get on your boss's case, or cases, by keeping track of her calendar schedule.

For a legal secretary, conservative values and outfits are essential. Blue or gray business suits contrast perfectly with yellow legal pads. Fun and fads don't fit in well in most law firms, so never let on that you prefer reading *People* magazine to boring law journals.

Many legal secretaries improve their skills and gain knowledge in the field by serving as apprentices, paralegal aides, or watching *L.A. Law*. You may even choose to become the next Susan Dey or Perry Mason by turning to law school—or acting school.

The Medical Secretary

As a medical secretary you'll have the opportunity to bait and catch a doctor or to breathe and catch any number of maladies brought into the office by germ-ridden patients. You'll also have the chance to be at the receiving end of a nurse's condescending attitude.

Should you work for several doctors in a medical facility, you'll have the honor of scheduling, rescheduling, and re-rescheduling patients' appointments around doctors' golf games. This part of your job may not be as easy as it sounds, especially with Mrs. Robert Rogers calling you to schedule an appointment to see Dr. Finch the Podiatrist right after Mr. Roger Roberts called to schedule an appointment to see Dr. Flinch the Proctologist.

Your job will also require that you know how to read doctors' illegible scribbles and understand medical terminology. Naturally, nurses will gladly correct you should you make a mistake. Family and friends will discuss their ailments with you for the sole purpose of hearing you use your new wealth of medical jargon. Telling your uncle that you think he has acute halitosis will probably prompt a response from your aunt that she thinks he has a cute hell-of-a-whatsis too, but nevertheless, they'll be proud of you.

The successful medical secretary should have a sympathetic attitude toward physical illness and be able to uphold a patient's confidentiality, at least in the office. Since you may be asked to take down and type up patients' past medical histories, you must learn to refrain from responding to graphic medical descriptions with phrases like "That's disgusting," "Please don't touch anything on my desk," or "Gross!"

Occasionally, a medical secretary is asked to sterilize instruments or prepare a patient for examination. It is not proper to sterilize something by dunking it into the boiling water before putting in the teabag. Also, should you see an undressed patient prior to an examination, it is not your place to suggest a good spa at which he could lose some of that excess blubber.

Finally, should you decide to date a patient, you're in a great position to find out his complete medical history, not to mention health insurance and life insurance coverage. If you decide to date a doctor, you'll always know when the next available "free hour" will be.

The Male Secretary

Despite the fact that the vast majority of secretaries are female, male secretaries and temporary office workers do exist. Often Mr. Secretary will prefer to be called Mr. Assistant to avoid being thought of as "out of place" in the secretarial environment.

A great many assumptions are made about male secretaries. Some people assume they must be gay, others are convinced that a male secretary is either gunning for an executive position, a skirt chaser, or a Soviet spy.

It's important that a male secretary have a sense of humor, because he'll get a lot of ribbing for being a part of a female-dominated profession. It's also a good idea for a male secretary to have excellent skills, since he has to prove to a prospective employer that his motives are legitimate. He then has to prove it to the rest of the office.

A male temp confuses practically everyone. Even if the boss is fully aware that a temp will be outside her office at 9 a.m. sharp, the boss will ask the unknown male temp who he is and what he's doing there. Male temps face a variety of embarrassing moments, such as when they reach into their "desk for the day" and accidentally pull out a pair of pantyhose, or when the regular secretary's new flame calls up and coos to his "Angel Cake" before the temp even gets to say hello.

If a cute male temp appears to need a hand, he'll get more than he could ever dream of. If a "cool" male temp comes on like Mr. Playboy, his coworkers will turn his "coolness" to ice by giving him the cold shoulder. Thus the male temp has to watch his manners.

Most male secretaries and temps are simply guys who want to make a living in the business world, just like you. There are, however, those exceptions who want to dip into your nail polish, borrow your outfits, or fill your shoes.

Office Temps

Nomads of the Secretarial World

If anonymity is what you want, then temporary office work is for you. No matter how you introduce yourself, you are known as "The Temp." If you're lucky, an employee might have owned a dog or known a bully in the second grade with the same given name, and you will therefore be known as Peter the Temp, or Kathleen the Temp. Last names for temps simply do not exist.

Temps are generally regarded as outsiders who aren't to be trusted. Despite the fact that you—"The Temp"—may very well be part of the same company, once you enter a certain department, you are looked upon as an alien being. Immediately your "coworkers" will pull their purses closer to their seats, cover their work, hide their Cross pens, move their coats to a place in constant view, and cease all personal conversations. One of the most familiar phrases overheard by a temp is "Never mind, I'll tell you about it later."

Most temps have better-than-average skills—and a wide variety of them. One skill often expected of this species is that of mind reader. Bosses are well known for expecting "The Temp" to know where the files are, who the important callers are, and how they like their morning coffee, before they even step out of the elevator.

Quite often "The Temp" becomes valuable, in that she is asked by everyone within earshot (and a few by intercom) to do any number of odious office chores. Cleaning out the coffeepot, stapling seven hundred reports together, or Xeroxing the last twenty-three years of back files are tasks that some feel a temp is made for. Others use temps for more practical purposes, such as taking abuse, or (in advertising) an occasional human sacrifice for the sake of pleasing a client.

Befriending "The Temp" often puts you on the office blacklist. Nonetheless, some fairly new employees (the same ones who once nursed a sickly robin back to health, and were polite to substitute teachers in grade school) will befriend "The Temp" at the risk of aliening the entire office. They might even go so far as to offer "The Temp" a piece of cake from the office birthday party, to which everyone but the lonely temp was invited.

Life for a temp isn't all bad, however. "The Temp" can always keep one comforting thought in mind: "I never have to see these people again." Temps can therefore enjoy a variety of jobs, without having to make a commitment. It's the office version of the swinging bachelor, or bachelorette (a word culled from *The*

Dating Game) lifestyle, and it's safer. "The Temp" is also not subjected to those tedious mandatory office meetings and has a built-in excuse for any, and all, errors: "I didn't know it was supposed to be done that way." This will work in most circumstances, but will need to be said with a great deal of conviction after filing John Williams under *J*.

Many temps are actually struggling actors, actresses, singers, law students, lion tamers, or chinchilla ranchers, just waiting for their big break to occur. Others are checking out the place for future employment, hiding from the law, or keeping busy until the baby is due.

Whatever their goals, and whoever they are, temps play an important role filling in for misplaced, very pregnant, or vacationing employees. They sit at your desk, rearrange your photos, and keep lists of those people who treated them with the utmost disrespect.

Every now and then, however, it just so happen that a temporary office worker does a job worthy of permanent employment. If this happens in your office, be sure you're not the one who made "The Temp" polish the elevator doors, or someday you may wake up and find that you were born a temp in your next life.

In Your Drawers: *Deep Dark Desk Secrets*

For a secretary, the desk is essentially a home away from home. It is the only place to "keep your things." You can tell a lot about a secretary by examining her desk drawers.

Here are a few things you might find:

Footwear: Either comfortable shoes for walking home, sneakers for the evening aerobic class, extra pairs of shoes for when a heel breaks, or dress shoes for when you receive a last-minute dinner date. Often a desk drawer will resemble a Thom McAn store.

Extra pantyhose: For those days when your running around causes runs.

Ties: (Male secretaries) For those days when you ate spaghetti with tomato sauce for lunch.

(Female secretaries) For those days when your boss attempted to open a bottle of Wite-Out and accidentally whited out the red tie you bought him for Christmas.

Photographs: Of family members, friends, pets, and one of your boyfriend, girlfriend, or spouse, that's not quite suitable for framing. This picture helps you get through the slow hours during the day.

Gum: Because chewing helps you maintain your typing rhythm.

Magazines: Always folded back to a half-read article, a crossword puzzle, a self-improvement quiz, or the personal ads.

Greeting cards: Usually Christmas cards given to you by coworkers two or three years ago, or studio cards too filthy to send to anyone.

Unfinished "work": Those extra memos that should have been filed years ago, and those letters that you forgot to send out last month.

Sunglasses: For outdoor lunching during summer, looking cool, or hiding those bloodshot eyes from last night's party.

An umbrella: You always remember it's there once you're outside getting wet, but you rarely bother to go back and get it.

Cookies and candy: Hard as rock from being there for six months.

Nail file/nail polish/nail polish remover: For when that damn typewriter destroys one of your nails.

Menus: When the big decision of the day arises—where to order lunch from—you're always ready. Your menu selections offer a variety of international cuisine at affordable prices. Sometimes, however, you may think twice before ordering from Joe's House of Eggrolls & Blintzes.

Shopping bags: To carry home birthday gifts, Christmas gifts, office supplies, packages from your lunch-time shopping spree, or all of the above items in your desk should your job abruptly come to an end.

Favorite Foods

The secretarial menu is well chosen to include high-energy foods, as well as low calorie consumption. Here are some secretarial favorites:

Yogurt. The best thing about yogurt, besides being nonfattening, is that it slides down and won't get stuck in your throat when your boss yells. It's also easy to eat when talking on the phone.

Tuna or chicken salad. Popular simply because they're hard for most cafeterias and coffee shops to screw up.

Bagels, muffins, and croissants. These morning goodies arc not only inexpensive, but give you some morning exercise as you spread an assortment of butters, jellies, and cream cheese on them.

Salads. The chief reason for eating salad is that it produces "natural gas" that will keep your boss or anyone else from looking over your shoulder while you work.

Fruit. Good for eating, and ideal for throwing at the right person.

Melba toast. Good low-calorie bread substitute, also ideally suited for bookmarks.

Free-Time Challenges

Here are a few fun things you might try to do with your few moments of free time throughout the day:

1. Try to break Stella Pajunas Garnand's 1946 typing record (according to the *Guinness Book of World Records*) of 216 WPM This doesn't mean typing the words "I" and "A" 108 times each.
2. Begin making the longest paper-clip chain in the world, and add to it daily.
3. Type an erotic memo to that secret somebody in the office that you'd kill for, then be sure to throw it out.
4. Use your calculator to add up the approximate ages of everyone in the office, then divide to find the average. If you're way above it, spend the next hour figuring out what your pension will be and how soon you can get it.
5. Surreptitiously push your desk one inch closer to the one across the aisle from you. If you have an overweight boss, you may try doing this everyday until one morning she is unable to fit between them and freaks out.
6. Tape a plastic fish to the back of the watercooler and watch people's first reactions as they peer through the glass, thinking they have a swimming visitor.
7. Tape a photo of your face to a picture in *Playboy* magazine, Xerox it, and leave a copy on your desk until someone notices it.

PART 5

Basic Skills

An Ode to Typing

Your grade point average was 3.4.
You had a most impressive SAT score.
You breezed through college like smoke through a pipe.
But all they want to know is "Can you type?"

On the social scene you can dance up a storm.
In your sleep you can file and keep coffee warm.
You find difficult financial reports easy to read.
But all they want to know is your typing speed.

You know karate, and Yoga, and CPR.
For graduation you were given a fancy car.
There are three foreign languages in which you can rap.
But all they care about is how accurately you tap.

You've read Shakespeare, and Tolstoy, and Chaucer, too.
You can find a missing item with a single clue.
You could run the whole damn office with apparent ease.
But all they care to know is how fast you can hit those keys!

Oh, Those Flying Fingers

In the secretarial world, Typing is next to Godliness. The speed at which you can hit those keys is the key to your success. The modern typewriter, or word processor, can eliminate mistakes; unfortunately it can't stop you from making them in the first place.

To be a good typist you should know your typewriter. You might even choose to name your typewriter. Choose a friendly name like Sam, Edna, or perhaps Betty. This way you can spend your time working with Betty from Olivetti, or you can tell your friends that you couldn't take your hands off of Sam all day. This may cause people to wonder what it is that you actually do for a living. You should also know how your typewriter works. Learn how to change the ribbon, how to set the margins, and most important how to put the cover over it when you can't figure out why every time you hit an F you get a W. Then try explaining to your boss why a letter to Mr. John Feeny reads: to Mr. John Weeny.

Correct typing posture is also very important to good typing. Proper typing posture includes: planting your feet on the floor and sitting up tall, with your stomach in, arms straight, head up, knees bent, eyes down, mouth slightly open, fingers curved, chin down, spine straight, ears back, and thumbs one inch apart. Remember that once you finally achieve proper typing posture, you should try not to get up from your seat for any reason during the remainder of the workweek.

To be an accurate typist you must concentrate, keep your eyes on the copy, and hope that your boss doesn't spell well enough to catch your mistakes. It's also a good idea not to talk on the phone while you type or your conversation could find its way into a business letter. The following is an example taken from an actual business letter:

"... and it is of great concern to the company, and the stockholders, that we go to a movie tonight. Maybe we could see the new Paul Newman picture since our gross assets are higher this quarter than they have been at any previous time this year. I would like to schedule a conference at about eight-thirty this evening after I am done washing my hair."

Sincerely,
Robert T. Walsh, V.P. Sales
See you later

In typing, rhythm means a smooth continuity of key tapping. You should establish a comfortable typing rhythm for yourself. Try to avoid a staccato or reggae beat, as you are likely to break up words in the wro ng pl ac es. Remember not to tell people that you use the rhythm method, or they're likely to misconstrue your statement.

Finally, it is important to remember that typing speed is a way of gaining status. In the Old

West respect was won by the fastest gun; in the office it's won by the fastest fingers.

Match your typing speed to the list below and see how you rate in the office:

- If you type over 80 words per minute, the boss does what you say while your coworkers cower in your presence. No one dares to cross you. Maintain a strong presence at all times, otherwise everyone who appreciates your skill will want you to do their work, since you can get it done so much faster. Always be on the lookout, because everyone is gunning (or typing) to get you.
- If you type 65 to 79 words per minute, you are respected, your opinion matters, and you are able to make up for any other office shortcomings by using your typing skills. Your only nemesis is a competitive 80 WPM typist. You are considered top deputy.
- If you type 55 to 64 words per minute, you are considered adequate, average, sufficient—and replaceable—so you had better be on your toes and smile a lot. Your coworkers are behind you, because you are truly one of them—no better, no worse. Essentially you're "The most mediocre gun in the West, or typist in the office."
- If you type from 45 to 54 words per minute, you'd better make the meanest cup of coffee north of Brazil. Either that, or your mere presence and personality should light up the office, because you sure aren't setting any world records hitting those keys. Flaunt whatever else you can: intelligence, a sparkling smile, great legs, or a keen ability to blackmail somebody.
- If you type 35 to 44 words per minute, you're either doing something naughty with your boss, or you're the head honcho's kid. Essentially, you're the fastest gun in the West's best buddy, because someone's looking out for you. Be careful, however, because if your office supporter should fly the coop, you may also be gunned down (or pink-slipped) at high noon.
- If you type less than 35 words per minute, you're reading the wrong handbook.

Scheduling Appointments

A daily calendar for your desk, one for your executive's desk, a small pocket directory, one for your glove compartment, a cat calendar for the wall, and 365 dated daily index cards for your top drawer are basic to scheduling appointments. Some executives like to use the month-at-a-glance or year-at-a-glance calendars, while less secure execs stick to the hour-at-a-glance models.

First you should note all annual recurring conferences and meetings on your calendars. Next put a black *X* over the day on which you plan to leave if you haven't yet received a raise. Then place a double red line across the day on which you will "seriously" walk out if your cost of living increase has not yet been met. Put a yellow circle around your upcoming vacation week(s), and a gold star on your birthday.

Below are some other pointers regarding the scheduling of appointments:

1. When entering appointments on your calendars, be sure they are neatly written, clearly written, and written in pencil for when your boss, or the other party, changes them six or seven times.

2. If your employer has just returned from an out-of-town trip you should schedule only slow-talking, soft-spoken visitors to meet with him. This will allow your boss to catch a brief nap during the meeting.

3. Schedule appointments lightly on Monday mornings, Friday afternoons, before or after holidays, before or after three-martini luncheons, on the day of your next review, or the day your boss's divorce becomes official.

4. If you're scheduling an appointment, suggest a time that's convenient to yourself rather than asking "When would you like to meet?" This way you'll be able to insure that you will be able to greet the visitor and not be on a lunch date, getting a manicure, or taking a long lunch hour to finish an aerobic dancing class.

5. When scheduling appointments for certain executives, such as those who drink heavily, or those who are either moody or unreliable, it is often financially advantageous to bet against your coworkers (giving Las Vegas odds) on whether your boss will cancel or miss the meeting.

6. When scheduling an appointment for a visitor who is in the office, hand out a reminder card with the time and date of the meeting on it. If you have a personal interest in this individual, add your phone number and the best times you can be reached at home, and gently dab the card with perfume.

7. If someone is late for an appointment, call to see if he has forgotten the meeting. If he is regretfully unable to attend, check with your boss about rescheduling the appointment. If the other party has simply neglected to attend the meet-

ing and offers no credible or cleverly inventive excuse, then it is proper to reschedule the appointment for a time when your boss will be out of town. This will give the irresponsible other party a taste of his own medicine. If the other party is dead, do not reschedule.

8. Should your boss schedule appointments without telling you about them, you should scold him and refuse to greet the visitors.

9. If a visitor of the opposite sex has been especially rude to you, offer to walk him/her to the elevator. When a crowded elevator arrives, toss a pair of undies at him/her exclaiming, "I think these belong to you."

Dictational Rap

I hope you'll carefully get this down—
It's what I have to say.
Make sure it's typed up perfectly,
Then throw it all away.

I dictate letters all the time—
They're either short or long.
Problem is when you read them back,
I've said everything all wrong.

It's tough, you know, to be a boss—
How I got here I'm not sure—
But despite my lack of abilities,
They put my name on the door.

So all I ask as you take this down—
And I'll slip you an extra fee—
Is that you get my thoughts on the steno pad,
Then rewrite the letter for me.

Dictation

Taking It and Faking It

How to get the boss's ramblings on paper has long been a question pondered by many secretaries. Steno, which is now generally used to encompass shorthand, speed writing, or any other technique you may employ, is a secretary's way of keeping pace with the boss.

The official language of shorthand is considered by most secretaries to be Gregg shorthand. This is a system where each and every phonetic sound has a written equivalent. These circles and swirls, twists and twirls, create words.

Here are a few examples:

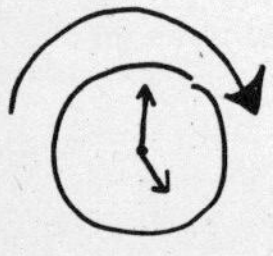

DO LUNCH

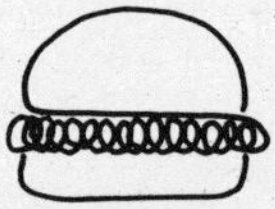

OVERTIME

VACATION PAY

FORMAL

WIFE (THE BOSS'S)

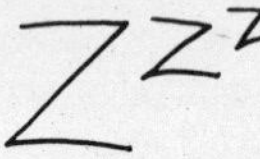

BOARD (BORED) MEETINGS

FUNDRAISING

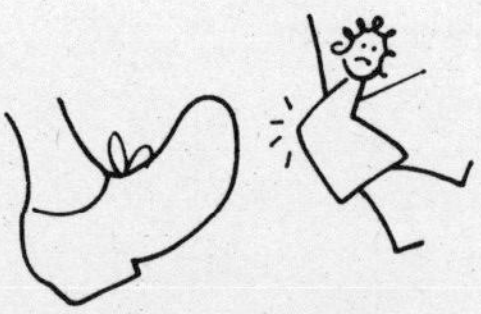

LAY OFF (OR FIRED)

SINCERELY

Taking Dictation . . .

While taking any form of dictation, you must keep pace with your boss. Knowing what word is likely to follow is good, but often a clever boss will try to outwit you. This makes dictation more of a challenge for both parties. Fake coughs, an occasional sneeze, or perhaps looking abruptly at the door or window will break your boss's train of thought, giving you time to catch up. Should you fall significantly behind, you might try yelling "Fire," knocking over his cup of coffee, or falling off your chair. Crossing your legs seductively may slow a male boss down, while humming should distract and annoy any boss.

Another hazard of taking dictation is the stuttering, stammering, or editing boss. To deal with the first two, you must simply slow down a bit. The last one, however, is a killer. The editing boss is constantly changing words that you took down moments ago. Here is a short dialogue between an editing boss and his secretary:

BOSS: . . . and it should also be known that my first choice would be to send the third script to the party of the second part . . . no, no, make that my third choice would be to send the second script to the party of the first part. Read that back to me.

SECRETARY: . . . and my third choice would be to send the second script to the party of the first part.

BOSS: Make that third part.

SECRETARY: Make what third part?

BOSS: Make first part third part, and make that my second choice.

SECRETARY: You mean it should read . . . and my second choice is to send the second script to the party of the third part?

BOSS: No no, that's not my second choice. I'd make that my first choice.

SECRETARY: You'd make what your first choice?

BOSS: Aren't you getting this down?

SECRETARY: Certainly.

BOSS: Good, then let me see what you've got.

SECRETARY: I beg your pardon?

BOSS: Written down.

SECRETARY: My first choice would be to send the second script to the party of the third part.

BOSS: How does that sound to you?

SECRETARY: Fine, sir.

BOSS: What does it mean?

SECRETARY: I have no idea.

BOSS: Do you think they'll understand it?

SECRETARY: I honestly doubt it.

BOSS: Good, then send it.

. . . *And Faking Dictation*

Should you become confused when trying to read your own scribble, use discretion. It's usually acceptable to ask your boss to repeat a word, but a paragraph or two may be overdoing it. Try substituting the word you think your boss *would* have said. Words like "nifty," "groovy," or phrases like "get down" are not commonly used by lawyers or CPAs and it is unlikely that your boss would fail to miss this substituted word on your part.

All things considered, the best scenario is the one where the boss dictates his message onto a tape player and you play it back. Some bosses have a great deal of fun using this method and may even throw in a comment directed at you as they dictate. For example, one boss dictated thc following:

> "In closing, I would like to applaud your efforts at securing the Madison account, and while I'm giving out praise, I'd like to thank you, Debbie, for those cookies you made last week . . . they were great. Anyway, back to the letter . . ."

If your boss doesn't choose to use a machine you can always fake dictation. This is done by appearing to take dictation, while keeping a miniature tape recorder running someplace on your person, or in your nearby handbag. You can then gladly type up the letter while playing your Walkman. Should your boss insist that you not wear your Walkman in the office, you will need one super-long trip to the ladies' room to transcribe.

TO WHOM IT MAY CONCERN
A Quiz on Business Letters

1. An appropriate salutation for a letter directed to a member of the clergy might be:
- A. Dear Father Smith:
- B. Hi, Father:
- C. Forgive Me, Father, for I Have Sinned:

2. A letter marked CONFIDENTIAL means:
- A. The letter contains information that requires protection because its unauthorized disclosure could prove to be damaging to one or more persons.
- B. It should be posted on the company bulletin board, or copied immediately for blackmail purposes.
- C. Your boss is having an affair.

3. Federal Express:
A. Delivers letters in 24 hours.
B. Loses letters in 15 minutes.
C. Is a laxative for politicians.

4. Which would appear to be appropriately addressed?
A. The Merico Corporation
443 Merico Drive
Los Angeles, Ca. 91365
B. The Merico Corporation
443 Merico Drive
Los Angeles, Ca., USA, North America, Earth, 91365
C. The Merico Corporation
Somewhere on Merico Street or Drive
It's a big white building in L.A., you can't miss it.

5. If your boss asks you to sign the letter for him:
A. You either sign his name or use his stamp.
B. You sign your name and leave a fingerprint.
C. You read the letter back to him in sign language.

6. An appropriate, friendly, but not too personal close would be:
A. Sincerely, or Sincerely Yours
B. Bye Bye, or Ta Ta.
C. I like you, but only as a friend.

7. Business letters should be sent on:
A. Office or company stationery.
B. Personal or flowery stationery.
C. The back of old memos or take-out menus.

8. A proper signature block for a business letter would be:
A. James P. Mason, Director.
B. James P. Mason, My Boss.
C. Pat Smith, Secretary to James P. Mason.

Office Etiquette

- Never trust a boss who calls you for dictation and asks you to bring a pencil, notepad, and bottle of champagne.
- If your boss or office pal, whose confidence you have not yet

gained, is coming to your home, always remember to tidy up by hiding a few things such as: the office stapler you ordered for yourself in canary yellow; the matching forty to fifty yellow memo pads adorning your desk; the typewriter that was reported "stolen" some months ago; that cute little electric pencil sharpener you couldn't resist; and the old filing cabinet that "had to be replaced anyway, since it was the wrong color."

- Keep in mind that if your coworkers throw you a surprise "going away party," things don't look too good for your promotion.
- While an occasional personal visitor may be permitted within your work area, whole families, party groups, or gangs (especially the street variety) aren't usually welcome.

Pointed Pointers for Secretaries

Here are some rules of thumb formulated specially for you, your boss' right hand:

1. Avoid clipping your toenails at your desk.
2. Try to learn how to work the intercom as opposed to shouting at people across the office or throwing paper airplane messages.
3. Do not refer to your boss as "Yo" unless you work for Yo Yo Ma or Sylvester Stallone.
4. Eat simple things at your desk, such as yogurt as opposed to ribs, finger sandwiches as opposed to meatball heroes, a small salad as opposed to spaghetti.
5. If you choose to play a radio, play it softly and listen to something your coworkers can also appreciate. Don't blast Bon Jovi and dance on your desk . . . unless you work for a radio station.
6. If you walk in and interrupt your boss talking on the phone, you should apologize and leave. Clutching the chair leg, weeping uncontrollably, and screaming "Dear God forgive me!" is generally considered overreacting, unless you work for an advertising agency.
7. At a meeting it is polite to offer everyone coffee, not just those whom you think might leave you a tip.
8. Never serve baked beans at board meetings.
9. Don't wear a rubber finger to stir coffee.
10. Don't use a spray can to write graffiti on the elevator door. (Use a Magic Marker.)

11. Never let the phone ring more than eighteen times before answering it, unless you know for sure that it's an insurance salesman.

12. Avoid doing anything in your office that Howie Mandel would do.

13. When your boss is interviewing a job applicant, you should refrain from snickering.

14. Don't wear your Walkman during important meetings.

15. When ordering office supplies, avoid putting death threats on the order form (even though it could help you receive your supplies before the end of the decade).

PART 6

Basic Equipment and Scenery

Copiers

A good copier is defined as one that doesn't break down five minutes before your lunch hour.

Copiers come in all sizes and are equipped with a plethora of modern features. The latest Japanese import can collate, separate, enlarge, reduce, seduce, print both sides of the page, print in nine colors, translate into four foreign languages, and toast bagels or bran muffins.

Unfortunately, copiers need paper—and someone to feed it to them. Since the copier in a busy office needs to be fed more often than a six-month-old, some lucky secretary finds herself playing mommy to this technological brat. For confused secretaries with children at home, here are the differences:

INFANTS	COPIERS
Need frequent feedings.	Need an endless supply of paper.
Need clean diapers.	Need a clean paper tray.
Drink a lot of formula.	Drink an unlimited amount of toner. (Nobody actually knows what toner is.)
Need to be burped so they won't choke.	Need to have their paper path cleared so they won't get backed up.
Need pediatricians.	Need repairmen. (Who charge more than pediatricians.)
Signal you by crying.	Signal you by beeping.

A Glossary of Other Office Machines

Adding Machine
Adds numbers quickly, and keeps a running tape. It usually runs out of tape before you finish and is generally found on the desk of someone you really don't want to work around.

Copier
It has more working parts than a Boeing 747 and is designed to make copies of business material such as recipes, newspaper articles, movie time schedules, and dirty cartoons. Also designed to break down six to eight times a week. Easily the most hated and most often kicked machine in any office, after the candy-vending machine.

Stapler
Designed to put two or more pieces of paper together while breaking your nail or hurting your hand from excessive pounding. Also designed to jam or run out of staples at 4:57 P.M. when you have just one more item to go.

Dictaphone
The original Walkman, except instead of listening to "The Boss" Bruce Springsteen, you get stuck listening to *your* boss. Dictaphones are designed to make your boss even less intelligible than usual.

Calculator
Quick, compact adding device used mainly to figure out the cost of your next vacation, how much tax is taken out of your paycheck, how much you could have saved on lunch, how many calories you've had today, and for balancing your checkbook. Easily lost . . . or ripped off.

Office Landscaping

How to Turn Your Cubicle into a Tropical Paradise

You spend eight or more hours per day in your office environment, and you should have the right to make these surroundings as pleasant as possible, right? Since most office spaces are drab and utilitarian at best and claustrophobic and downright ugly at worst, and since most bosses' interest in their secretaries' accommodations consists of providing them with a place to sit while they type, it's up to you to landscape and decorate your own work space.

Here are some distinctive interior decorating styles that can be handily adapted to an office environment. Choose the one that suits your own inner self, and see how much faster the workday goes when you're living inside your own private fantasy!

Contemporary Cuteness

While Wall Streeters and corporate lawyers may scoff outwardly at this motif, they may well respond inwardly to the comforting, cartoony ambience—even to the point of grabbing and hugging one of your stuffed animals after a particularly stressful day. To create cuteness in your cubicle, adorn the "walls" with a cat calendar and other feline photos. Colorful Crayola drawings of houses, stick figures, fire engines, or boats done by your own child, or nephew or niece, also lend a nice touch. Decorate your desk with happy faces on the In Box, "Have a Nice Day" drinking mugs, miniature Snoopy statuettes, and tiny stuffed Alfs. Finally, you need a few adorable Disney character erasers to put on your pencils, two or three mushy greeting cards, and several Rolodex-style photo holders for your guests to flip through. (Be sure to include photos of yourself as a child, and every pet you've ever had.) Larger stuffed animals and Storybook dolls of the countries you've visited or hope to visit can adorn your shelves, along with a game of Candyland, to complete the homy, stressless atmosphere.

High Trek

Smooth white-and-silver Contac walls, resembling a space station interior, are the first steps to creating the High Trek look. A sleek combination digital clock-radio-TV-calculator-telephone should be the only item on your desk, which should resemble a black monolith as closely as possible (they're doing wonders with molded plastic these days). Your top-of-the-line IBM computer terminal should sit below a light built directly into the wall, which nobody has any idea how to turn off. Every decorative item, especially your stainless steel planet mobile, should reflect brightly enough to be used as a mirror. A light-up map of the universe adorns your wall (if any). The idea is to create an atmosphere so businesslike and yet so terrifyingly sterile that not even your boss will venture into it to bother you. For this reason, it might be feasible to incorporate a ceiling tanning device.

Classic Caribbean

With a little reggae or calypso music in the background, a slew of tropical plants obscuring the cubicle walls, and seashells used as a doorstop and as ashtrays and paper clip holders, you can turn your office into a tropical hideaway. Travel posters of the islands are perfect for the walls, and some sand on the floor enhances the island atmosphere, especially if your boss allows you to go barefoot. Piña coladas should replace your daily cups of coffee, with tiny umbrellas substituted for stirrers. Above your head should be a ceiling fan, and on your desk a stuffed iguana. Real reptiles may tend to elicit

screams from your coworkers. Finally, if you keep the temperature at a comfortable ninety-two degrees, anyone who walks in, including your boss, will soon join you in your afternoon siesta. This decor also lends itself well to the inclusion of a tanning device.

Oriental Flavor

To set the proper tone you must first replace the drab cubicle "walls" that surround your "space" with beautiful Oriental screens. Instead of a traditional office chair behind a desk, you might also enjoy moving your office equipment to the floor, where you can work while sitting on comfortable pillows. A nice kimono, a desk fan, and bare feet will create the proper ambience. It may also attract strange looks from coworkers and visitors, not to mention your boss. Your desk lamp should be replaced by a lantern or two, and your afternoon cup of coffee shall now be your afternoon tea. Most important, however, you must remember not to suggest bathing with your boss or coworkers, and it's not advisable to eat yogurt at your desk with chopsticks. You might grow weary of your new Chinese typewriter. The latest model has 5,850 characters, offered at a rate of 11 words per minute.

Fun with Phones

A pleasant voice, tact, and fast fingers are the main qualifications needed to handle the telephone efficiently.

Your objective in using the modern phone system is to put as many people on hold as possible. To do this, you must keep taking incoming calls on lines two through ten while continuing a lengthy conversation on line one.

Once you start taking your collection of waiting callers off hold, you should be as poised and polite as possible. You must now quickly decide the importance of each caller. Does your boss really want to speak to her ex-spouse? Is there any logical reason to put through a call from someone seeking a secretarial job? Is the president of the company really on line three, or is it an imposter? Does your boss have any earthly reason to speak with a politician? These are the questions you have to ask yourself. Your only ally is the hold button, which you can use in the event that you need more decision-making time. Perhaps you can decide over lunch while the caller holds.

It is of the utmost importance that you sound friendly and interested in whatever the caller has to say. Avoid chewing in the caller's ear, and never use phrases like: "Not you again!" or "What is it this time?"

Placing calls is a foolish but necessary job. It's foolish simply because it takes your boss more time to tell you to call someone than it would take for her to make the call herself. It's necessary because anyone with a secretary wants it known that she doesn't have to do such menial things as dial a telephone.

Push-button phones make it easy to reach the secretary of the intended receiver. They also make it easy to accidentally reach a non-English speaking mechanic in a distant area code. It's important to recognize a misdialed call before putting your boss on the line. That way you can avoid the following scenario:

OTHER PARTY: Vinnie's.

SECRETARY: Good morning, Mr. Perkins of Commodore Incorporated calling, one moment please.

YOUR BOSS: Pete, I presume you got Ann Clover's report?

OTHER PARTY: You wanna pie with anchovies?

YOUR BOSS *(Laughing)*: You've got a great sense of humor, Pete Green, I love it!

OTHER PARTY: Green olives we don't got.

YOUR BOSS: C'mon Pete, have you been hitting the sauce?

OTHER PARTY: You want extra sauce? C'mon I'm busy!

YOUR BOSS *(Laughing)*: All right, Pete, just look over Ann Clover's report and get it back to me as soon as possible. I think this could really mushroom into something large.

OTHER PARTY: Okay, we send a large pie with anchovies, mushrooms, and extra sauce as soon as possible.

(Twenty minutes later)

YOUR BOSS: Who ordered a pizza?

You should also remember that when you do reach the correct intended party, it becomes the job of both secretaries to get their bosses on the line at approximately the same moment. This will prevent your boss from (God forbid) having to wait for the other party to respond.

Transferring calls to other parts of the office is exciting because in most offices you usually have no idea whether the call actually ever got to its destination or not. The main objective during call transference is to create as many clicking noises in the caller's ear as possible. Sometimes it's fun to team up with your coworkers and transfer a call around the office six or eight times. This is a most effective way to eliminate a frustrating, unimportant caller such as: an office equipment salesman, a customer with a complaint, anyone taking a survey, a heavy breather, or an ex-boyfriend. Sometimes you can make a game out of it, the object being to pass the call to every secretary on the floor without hitting the same secretary twice.

The toughest job, however, in dealing with office phones is covering, or filling in for, the receptionist. Each call must be answered as quickly as possible, with the name of the company given. Unfortunately, certain companies have rather lengthy names, and you will find yourself shortening the name as the day goes by. Thus after eighty-nine calls The Royce, Allen, Paine, and Therbutt Company becomes The Royal Pain in the Butt Company.

Other Uses for Office Equipment

Here are a few new things to do with those humdrum items you find around your desk:

1. Smear butter on the roller of your typewriter to handily butter corn on the cob.
2. Use a staple remover to pierce your coworker's ears. (Two holes per ear!)
3. Spin a Rolodex rapidly enough to create an acceptable desk fan.
4. Use old typewriter ribbons to wrap gifts for people who don't mind getting their hands dirty.
5. Use two pencils as chopsticks to eat your Chinese take-out food.
6. Use your In Box as a bassinet for your infant on those days you can't get a baby-sitter.

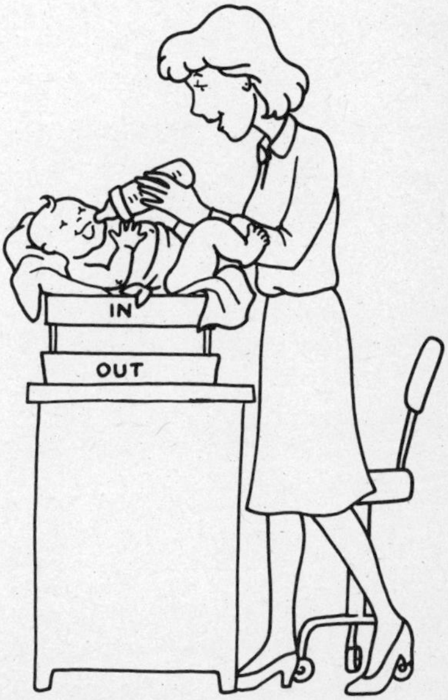

7. Use a very full file drawer to press shirts between the company files.

8. Slice the ice cream cake at your birthday party with a letter opener.

9. Use the blue ink from your stamp pad for eye shadow.

10. Use chains of paper clips on your whitewall tires for better traction in the snow.

11. Use your computer disk drive to heat pieces of toast.

PART 7

Daily Routines

Odd Jobs

"You Want Me to Do What?"

Applying for a job usually means informing your potential employer of your secretarial skills. There are, however, other skills you may be called upon to use. Letting it be known immediately that "you don't do windows" is a good idea. And just because your boss was fool enough to throw a paper airplane and get it stuck in the ceiling just prior to a meeting with the chairman of the board is no reason why you should be the one to climb up on the filing cabinet to retrieve it. Weighing less than your boss has nothing to do with it.

"I love the way you do your hair," was the compliment Ms. Tempkin paid her secretary at a small real estate company in Hartford, Connecticut. This mere compliment led to a discussion that revealed that Cathy (Ms. Tempkin's secretary) styled her own hair, and the hair of some of her friends. Unfortunately this discussion led to a request for her to do Ms. Tempkin's hair. Cathy, feeling obligated, did Ms. Tempkin's hair, and now works for a middle-aged man in Woodbury, Connecticut. She finds this situation more relaxing, since her boss is bald.

The preceding story is just one example of a boss taking advantage of his secretary. Bosses have been known to request the bizarre and often impossible. Why should you blow up sixty-five balloons for his son's birthday party when he's the one who's full of hot air? It is your responsibility to ask your boss what qualifies you to attend his nine-year-old son's piano recital in his place, before you refuse. You may also question why you are expected to taste his lunch before your boss, the politician, eats it. You may also refrain from buying certain items, since you probably don't know where to purchase an office spittoon anyway.

A boss in Wisconsin once requested that his secretary wash his sports car. Noting that the car was parked directly below his office window, she simply took the pot of water boiling for tea and tossed it out the window and onto the automobile. Although her boss wasn't pleased, he did appreciate the humor of her response, until he realized that he had left his sunroof open.

Buying tickets for your boss can also pose problems. Is the middle mezzanine better than a private box at the theater? Are seats behind second base good at the ballpark? Buying a book of seating plans for local theaters and arenas is often a good idea. Buying extra tickets for a popular event and scalping them is an even better idea. If this is illegal where you live, however, you'd better set some petty cash funds aside for bail money.

Planning and scheduling business trips for your boss may be part of your duties. Going along to Hawaii might be a fringe benefit, but scouting around for your boss to see an active volcano is definitely not part of the job description. Sharing quarters with your boss is a definite no-no, even if you are both of the same sex, heterosexual, and in separate beds. The last thing you want showing up on your upcoming review are your personal hygiene habits. "Among Barbara's weaknesses are gargling loudly when others are trying to sleep, snoring, and clipping her toenails during *The Tonight Show*."

Often it is just your opinion that's requested. In the case of whether your boss should go to the Halloween party as Tarzan or Rambo, voicing an opinion might be fun. But what makes your opinion more valuable than Siskel and Ebert's when it comes to selecting which movie the bachelor boss and his newfound babe should see? You might suggest *Benji*, since it's probably at her level.

No matter what you're asked to do, remember that if it doesn't fall into strict secretarial guidelines, it may be to your advantage to bow out gracefully. Being asked if you think your boss should have a vasectomy is a bit beyond the limit. On the other hand, if you want to get back at him for not giving you that long-awaited raise, this might be the perfect opportunity to get him where it hurts!

The Top Ten Questions You'd Love Answered

1. Why do copier company representatives usually show up to fix the copier wearing a suit and tie?
2. Isn't it odd that lost delivery boys always end up at your desk asking for directions?
3. Why is it that travel and expense reports never have all of the receipts?
4. Why do you always get in the same elevator at 5:00 P.M. with the man whose foot your high heel pierced on your 9:00 A.M. elevator ride?
5. How come, whenever you open a bottle of Wite-Out, hundreds of dried up little white particles spill all over your papers?
6. Why do office supply salesmen promise you gifts if you buy more supplies than your office could ever possibly need?
7. Why is it that after you've made sixteen business calls, your boss will walk by during your only personal call of the day?
8. Why does your boss always come in and complain how bad business has been on the day you were planning to approach him with a raise request?
9. Why are computers considered to be a step up in the business world when they're down so often?
10. Why are modern office buildings designed to have windows that don't open and air conditioners that break down?

Making Coffee

Wake Up and Smell the Cappuccino

It's 8:30, and you're the first one in the office. After hanging up your coat, it's time to prepare for the day. The first assignment is to make coffee, and plenty of it. To simplify your task, most offices are equipped with automatic coffee makers. These machines are so easy to operate that an executive can almost (but not quite) figure them out.

The necessary condiments are milk or a nondairy powdered creamer (better known as chalk dust) and sugar or a newfangled all-chemical substitute that is supposed to be healthier for you.

You must also have a large supply of Styrofoam or plastic cups with accompanying plastic holders. Of course, some executives are fortunate enough to have their own coffee mugs with adorable sayings such as "Boss," "Best Dad In The World," "Teddy Bear," or "Hug Me."

In order to keep the java flowing, or spinning, you'll also need a supply of stirrers. There's nothing sadder than seeing the president of a major corporation discreetly trying to stir his coffee with a number two pencil.

Finally, you must have a coffee filter—which can double as a party hat when needed—and a sufficient amount of coffee, both regular and decaffeinated. The former is for the hard-core caffeinees in the group, while the latter is for those too nervous to risk an artificial stimulant.

Now that you have all the ingredients, and a clean coffeepot, it's time to start brewing. If you're lucky, you'll end up with something between coffee-flavored soup and mud. If you're not lucky, perhaps you can talk everyone into turning British for a day and drinking tea.

Memos

Read Them and Weep

Memos are letters from one side of the office to the other. Here are a couple of office favorites:

TO: ALL PERSONNEL
FROM: MITCH LONDON, EXEC. V.P.
SUBJECT: PLANTS

Please be advised of the new policy regarding plants on individual desks. We realize that plants do enhance the decor of the office. However, we would appreciate your using discretion in choosing an appropriate-sized plant for an office. Several creeping Charlies and wandering Jews have crept and wandered their way into the president's private office. Currently the seventh floor greatly resembles a 1940s Tarzan film. Seven potted palms, three rubber trees, a couple of coconut trees, a baby redwood, plus a few hundred smaller varieties of foliage are making it virtually impossible for many executives to locate their secretaries.

We are also displeased with the recent practice of using the sprinkler system to water this wide assortment of office foliage.

Please make an effort to remove the larger plants in the near future, as our office has already been photographed for the cover of *Plant Life* magazine.

Thank you for your cooperation.

Mitch London,
Exec. V.P.

TO: Henry Greenberg
FROM: The Entire Secretarial Staff

The loyal and dedicated employees of Snippet Scissors Corp. would like to make what we feel is a reasonable and warranted request.

We would be grateful, as would our shoes and skirt hemlines, if the carpeting on our floor could be vacuumed at least once a week (it hasn't been vacuumed in ages). We find it quite embarrassing leaving a line of footprints from the building to our cars in the nearby lot.

When we first moved into this office we had lovely white carpeting beneath our feet. Now we are putting our collective foot down, and as we do a gray cloud rises from the floor. It has reached the point where a dropped paper clip is lost forever.

Thank you in advance for your cooperation.

The Secretarial Staff

Messages
While You Were Out

DATE: 8/24 TIME: 4:45
TO: Mr. P. W. Herman

WHILE YOU WERE OUT

MR. Rogers called
OF: Children's Television Inc.
PHONE: 123-4567

MESSAGE: Get out of the neighborhood!

DATE: 10/23 TIME: 11:30
TO: Mr. Barnum

WHILE YOU WERE OUT

MR. Chambers called
OF: Elephants R Us
PHONE: BIG-NFAT

MESSAGE: Just called to confirm that we are sending out your order for 21 well-trained elephants.

DATE: 11/24 TIME: Noon
TO: Mr. Palmer

WHILE YOU WERE OUT

MRS. Smith called
OF: Tryst Inc.
PHONE: (314) HOT-DATE

MESSAGE: That little luncheon appointment is all set. "Lunch" will be warming when you get there.

DATE: 6/23 TIME: 3:15
TO: Mr. Palmer

WHILE YOU WERE OUT

MRS. Palmer called
OF: His home life
PHONE (212) 174-2349

MESSAGE: Tell him his kids and his wife are considering putting his picture on milk cartons since we never see him anymore. If he's still alive have him call me!

DATE: 10/25 TIME: 11:45
TO: Mr. Jefferson

WHILE YOU WERE OUT

MS. Elizabeth called
OF: Buckingham Palace
PHONE: Unlisted

MESSAGE: Would appreciate it dearly if you would print a retraction on your story that Presley was her illegitimate son! Thank you.

DATE: 6/23 TIME: 1:25
TO: Mr. Palmer

WHILE YOU WERE OUT

MISS Peterson called
OF: He'll know
PHONE: He'll know

MESSAGE: He'll know, and tonight is fine!

DATE: 6/24 TIME: 11:35
TO: Mr. Palmer

WHILE YOU WERE OUT

MR. Segal, att'y-at-law, called
OF: Rosenberg, Sears, & Segal
PHONE: TRO-UBLE

MESSAGE: Wife had you followed. Is planning to take you to cleaners in divorce settlement. Have a nice day.

DATE: 3/26 TIME: 3:30
TO: Mr. Osteen

WHILE YOU WERE OUT

DR. Robinson called
OF: Cntr. for Behavioral Control
PHONE: 237-HELP

MESSAGE: I think the bed-wetting problem is significantly improved. Tell him to stop worrying about it so much.

DATE: 8/24 TIME: 2:00
TO: Mr. Simmons

WHILE YOU WERE OUT

MR. Wouldn't give name
OF: Wouldn't give location
PHONE: He'll call you back

MESSAGE: Still holding wife hostage. Please meet ransom demands. Will settle for half. She's driving me crazy.

DATE: 10/23 TIME: 3:40
TO: Mr. Chambers

WHILE YOU WERE OUT

MR. Barnum called
OF: Barnum & Bailey Circus
PHONE: BIG-TOP1

MESSAGE: That was supposed to be 12 elephants. Returning 9, have no room. Sorry.

DATE: 10/23 TIME: 4:45
TO: Mr. Barnum

WHILE YOU WERE OUT

MR. Chambers called
OF: Elephants R Us
PHONE: BIG-NFAT

MESSAGE: Sorry P. T., but we have a no-return policy on elephants, so I'm gonna have to ship them back. Nothing I can do. Better make room.

DATE: 1/2 TIME: 9:00
TO: Mrs. Herbie Wickets

WHILE YOU WERE OUT

MR. Herbie Wickets called
OF: Paulson's Plumming
PHONE: She has it.

MESSAGE: I'm sorry, must have been drunk at the New Year's Party. Found out the minister was legit. Let's get annulment. Sorry about the inconvenience.

Know Your Mail

First-class mail: Regular mail—business letters, statements, bills, etc., etc., etc. Boring.

Second-class mail: Publications, newspapers, magazines, and other things to keep on your lap under your desk to read throughout the day. Crossword puzzles can be found!

Third-class mail: Your boss's glasses, which he left in Baltimore; his keys, which he left in L.A.; and lots of fun stuff like lingerie catalogs.

Fourth-class mail: Instantly tossable stuff . . . JUNK MAIL.

Hand-delivered mail (messengered mail): Mail that should have arrived by noon, but comes at 4:55 P.M. after having gone to five incorrect locations first.

Overnight mail services: The only way to get that letter, which you forgot to send last week, to its destination in time.

Certified mail: An excellent excuse to do some shopping on your way to the post office.

Interoffice mail: The slowest and least reliable way to send a message to someone sitting twenty-five feet away from you.

Computerized mail: Direct way of sending mail via computer. Takes the fun out of everything!

Questions You Wish You Didn't Have to Answer

1. Could you stay until 6:00?
2. Is the mail here yet?
3. Is the coffee ready yet?
4. Did you retype that letter yet?
5. Which line is my wife on?
6. Could you pick up one of those for my wife?
7. Is the copier still broken?
8. Is that report finished?
9. Can you take a letter?
10. Is that a personal call?
11. You're not going to lunch, are you?
12. How's the stock market doing today?
13. Are you seriously asking for a raise?
14. Why didn't you answer my page?
15. Can you come in at 8:15 tomorrow morning?

Riding in Style

Ordering a Limo

Do you work for a boss whose only mode of transportation is a car that is longer than your living room? If it is your job to call for the cars, here is a conversation you may find yourself involved in.

(Phone rings)

CAROL: Lincoln Limousines, this is Carol speaking, may I help you?

MARIE: Yes, this is Mr. Walter's office calling. He informed me that he's been waiting for a car downstairs for nearly fifteen minutes. Is it on its way?

CAROL: Hold on, let me check. (*Brief pause*) Our dispatcher says the car is waiting at the Forty-fifth Street entrance.

MARIE: We don't have a Forty-fifth Street entrance. That's our old office. We're now at Forty-seventh Street.

CAROL: I'll have them tell the driver, but we have Forty-fifth Street written down, and I believe Mr. Walter called in the reservation himself.

MARIE: That explains it, he never remembers that we moved. Hold on, he's on the phone again from downstairs. (*Brief pause*) Okay, no problem, he said he'll walk over.

CAROL: Guess again. The dispatcher realized the mistake and just sent the car to Forty-seventh Street.

MARIE: So now we've got Mr. Walter on the way to Forty-fifth Street, and the car coming here to Forty-seventh?

CAROL: We'll send the car back to Forty-fifth. (*Brief pause*)

MARIE: Okay, the car will meet him at the old meeting place on Forty-fifth?

CAROL: Right, he's driving back around.

MARIE: Guess what? My boss just returned because he forgot an umbrella.

CAROL: Hold on, I'll have them send the car back to Forty-seventh.

MARIE: Hold on, I'll tell him the car is on its way.
(Brief pause)

CAROL: Okay, the car will be waiting at your new meeting place on Forty-seventh Street in five minutes.

MARIE: Mr. Walter just informed me that he made a mistake, his meeting isn't until three o'clock.

CAROL: Do you want the car to wait?

MARIE: He said no, he'll take a cab.

CAROL: We're going to have to bill him.

MARIE: He doesn't care. *(Whispering)* He thinks he's rich.

CAROL: All right, I'll have them send the car elsewhere.

MARIE: Sorry about the mess.

CAROL: Don't worry, we're used to it.

(Ten minutes later. Phone rings.)

CAROL: Lincoln Limousine, can we help you?

MARIE: Hi, Carol, it's me again. Guess who wants the car again?

CAROL: You're kidding.

MARIE: I wish I were.

CAROL: Well, you're in luck, the car's still there.

MARIE: It is?

CAROL: Yeah, it stalled out. We're sending a truck to get it started.

MARIE: Great, I hear snoring coming from Mr. Walter's office. I'll go and make coffee to get him started, and with any luck . . .

CAROL: They'll both be ready at the same time.

Board Meetings, or Bored Meetings

How to Set Them Up, Stay Away, or Stay Awake

1. Find out where the meeting is supposed to be held and change the location ten to fifteen minutes prior to the meeting time. If you decide to leave well enough alone, be sure that all participants know the time and place. Frequent meeting locations include conference rooms, executive offices, executive washrooms, golf courses, overpriced, pretentious restaurants, company aerobics classes, and even a frequently stalled elevator.
2. Make sure all necessary supplies are on hand, including notepads, pens, pencils, No-Doz, daggers (for back stabbing), ashtrays, razor blades (for those people in the entertainment industry), hidden tape recorders, and possibly a shredder.
3. Be certain that all attendees know where the bathrooms are and how to use them. Also point out the watercooler, soda machine, and emergency exits in case anyone simply can't take it any longer. Do not indicate that there is a window ledge, or participants may be tempted to make use of it.
4. If asked to make coffee, make it strong, and be sure you're out of milk or cream so that you'll have an excuse to leave immediately to purchase a couple of quarts.
5. If asked to take the minutes of the meeting, suggest that your services might be put to better use answer-

ing the phones, or typing the letters that your boss left for you last week. If these polite methods fail, try hiccups, an allergic sneezing attack, cramps, or a lost contact lens. If you're still expected to take the minutes, do so, repeating each word aloud. Include who was snoring, and who was snickering. Remember minutes must accurately convey the tone of the meeting:

Present: Five out of eight board members were present: James Smith, Mark Wilson, Alex Peers, Carol Freed, and Nick Mason, who looked gorgeous in a new designer suit.

Absent: Jack Farrell, Andy Farrell, and Ned Farrell, who were either out playing golf or at a Farrell Family Reunion.

Report of the Chairman: The chairman, wearing a gray suit and red tie, reported on the growth in sales revenues during the last quarter, while Mr. Wilson and Mr. Peers played five riveting games of tic-tac-toe. Special attention was given to a new trade law involving importation taxes. At this point I glanced seductively at Mr. Mason.

Treasurer's Report: Mr. Smith, Treasurer, submitted the quarterly profit-and-loss statement. A somber mood overtook the meeting until Mr. Peers told a dirty joke about two English jockeys and a sheepdog. Miss Freed blushed. Mr. Smith then suggested that sufficient funds be appropriated to set up a cash liquor bar in the elevator. A vote was taken and the motion passed four to one.

Adjournment: After a ten-minute discussion of last night's Lakers-Celtics game, won by the Lakers in overtime, Miss Freed urgently made a motion for adjournment. The motion was seconded by yours truly, and since no one minded, the meeting was adjourned.

Sec'y and Other Abbreviations

A/C	account/air conditioning
A/C D/C	sexually confused
AP	accounts payable
AR	accounts receivable
ARL	account received but lost
ASAP	as soon as possible
ATE	already had lunch
BN	brown nose
BS	second office language
C	confidential
CC	carbon copy
CCC	Carol Channing's copy
CCCC	saying "yes" persistently in Spanish

C/O	care of
Co.	company
COA	cash on arrival
COB	chairman of the board
COD	cash on delivery/fish
COP	a police officer
CPA	certified public accountant/cleaning, pressing, and alterations
DP	data processor
DPsn	dull person
Encl.	enclosure
Ex. VP	executive vice-president
HWR	heads will roll
JR	character on *Dallas*
MBA	master of business administration
MBE	master of business embezzlement
No.	number
PC	petty cash
PG	petty gossip
PO	purchase order
POD	proof of delivery/ home for peas
SASE	self-addressed stamped envelope
T & E	travel and entertainment
T & SE	travel and sexual encounters
TGIF	thank God it's Friday
TS	top secret/Tom Selleck
VO	voucher
VP	vice-president
WB	we're Beatrice
WP	word processor
WPM	words per minute
WPY	words per year

Guarding the Boss

Your Role as a Protective Device

Despite the fact that it sounds like the name of an Arnold Schwarzenegger film, most secretaries find themselves in the role of the protector for their bosses. Here is a short list of situations from which a good secretary should be able to shield her boss.

Can you protect your boss from:

1. A protest rally led by the Hell's Angels?
2. His in-laws?
3. Two or three dozen dissatisfied stockholders?
4. An irate woman screaming something about a palimony suit?
5. Two men wearing dark suits and carrying violin cases?
6. A man named Lefty?
7. A pit bull?
8. The telephone company?
9. A persistent copier sales representative?
10. A gang of maniacal job applicants, bent on being interviewed?
11. A singing telegram delivered by someone in a gorilla suit?
12. An office Amway distributor?
13. The FBI?
14. Autograph seekers?

15. A competitive V.P. shouting something about stealing his idea?
16. The office tramp?
17. Geraldo Rivera looking for a story?
18. Robin Leach?
19. A disgruntled employee who has just snapped?
20. The revenge of his former secretary?
21. A junior reporter looking for some good "mis"quotes for a story?
22. A man disguised as a window washer whose sole intent is serving a subpoena?
23. A temp bent on working her way to the top immediately?
24. An insistent cleaning crew who refuses to accept the fact that your boss is working late?
25. An old army or high school buddy, who has just dropped by to "shoot the breeze for a while"?

If you answered YES to 20 or more of the preceding questions, you should be head of security at Fort Knox.

If you answered YES to 15 to 19 of the preceding questions, your boss should feel safe enough to throw away his security blanket.

If you answered YES to 10 to 14 of the preceding questions, your boss should at least feel that you're making an effort. He or she may well feel the need to change the locks on his or her office door and cabinets.

If you answered YES to 5 to 9 of the preceding questions, your boss has a justifiable reason for a drinking problem, and may be justified in installing a back "escape" door in the office.

If you answered YES to 4 or fewer of the preceding questions, your boss is a dead man!

Snack Time

Snack time can be almost any time of the day, especially in most large office buildings, where the cute little food cart comes around at least twice daily.

Food carts offer a variety of fruit, sandwiches, sodas, coffee, instant soups, and assorted junk that fits conveniently into your top desk drawer. The modern snack cart uses the Pavlovian theory, whereby a ringing bell causes the customers to start salivating. The modern secretary is trained to eliminate any phone calls or press the pause button on any Dictaphone immediately upon hearing the bell from the corridor. Since your boss will undoubtedly not hear the bell, or at least pretend not to hear it, it's up to you to offer your services as snack monitor. It's advised that you move quickly to beat the other contestants from neighboring offices in the race to the cart. Haste also diminishes your chance of becoming the junk food waitress for all of your "lazy" coworkers.

There are two things to keep in mind about snack carts:

1. The people who run them generally don't speak very much English. Quite understandably they may mistake a can of Slice for a can of Sprite, and they also tend to mix up words like "tuna sandwich" and "coffee cake." So speak slowly and clearly, and be repetitive.

2. Some of the food on the snack cart has been traveling the corridors of your building since 1963, so look over your selection very carefully.

Many offices do not have food carts or food trucks passing by, but do have the proverbial snack machines in the cafeteria. These machines operate on the same principle as Las Vegas slot machines, whereby you put in your coins, and if you're lucky, something comes out. If you are extremely lucky, you may even get the selection you pressed the button for.

Some machines have red squares that light up when a particular selection isn't available. Most machines are serviced so infrequently that the red lights are more plentiful than those on the company Christmas tree. Thus it is a good idea to approach the machine with at least seventeen choices of food in mind.

There are several things to remember about vending machines:

1. The coin return slot is generally the manufacturer's idea of a practical joke.

2. U.S. coins with pictures of Presidents on them are (for no explainable reason) not always acceptable in these machines.

3. Certain foods in the machine are no longer in production.

4. Food that is supposed to come in one piece may emerge from the machine in several pieces.

5. With your luck, it'll be *your* responsibility to call the repair person every Thursday when the machine breaks down.

Should those pangs of hunger strike when the snack wagon isn't available and the vending machines have nothing left to dispense, there is always one person to turn to in any busy office. This person, generally a chronic diet cheater (or fatty), hoards a considerable quantity of high-calorie edibles in her bottom desk drawer.

It is advisable always to be nice to this human fast food franchise in the event that you need a quick sugar or chocolate fix. After all, running a few hundred extra copies is worth a tasty treat anytime.

Watching this person eat lunch might be similar to watching a disaster movie with things flying in all directions, but should you be around in the aftermath, you may receive some good afternoon yummies. Half a sandwich, an extra piece of pie, or a Hostess cupcake will probably be available for the mere cost of typing a letter. You simply have to complain convincingly about your hunger pangs after a very unsatisfying lunch.

Remember, however, if you should find more food than work accumulating in your bottom desk drawer, then perhaps it's time to take a good look at yourself in the mirror . . . if all of you fits in the mirror!

MONDAY MORNINGS VS. FRIDAY AFTERNOONS

Monday Mornings	Friday Afternoons
You scowl as your boss reminds you to finish typing those letters you left on Friday afternoon.	You smile as your boss tells you to leave the rest of those letters for Monday morning.
You'd kill for a cup of coffee. "Why can't anybody else make coffee around here?"	You'd love to make a pot of coffee . . . "It's no trouble."
The ride to work is two hours longer than usual.	You can't believe how fast you got home.
You spend 9:00 to 11:00 A.M. recounting your weekend, until your boss tells you to get to work.	You spend 3:00 to 5:00 P.M. planning your weekend until your boss leaves and tells you to have a good one.
Nothing in the office works right!	No one in the office works right.

MONDAY MORNINGS VS. FRIDAY AFTERNOONS

Monday Mornings	Friday Afternoons
The telephone can ring six or eight times for all you care, since it's not for you anyway.	The telephone can't ring more then once, since it might be someone involved in your weekend plans.
Your boss is a slavedriver.	Your boss is a puppy dog.
The mail boy is a perverted little cretin.	The mail boy is a cute young stud.
The pile on your desk is a miserable two feet high.	You can't believe the pile on your desk is down to a mere twenty-four inches high.
The typewriter keys feel like lead weights.	You barely have to touch those keys to send them flying.
When your boss asks you to file a letter, you respond, "You wrote it, you file it."	You ask your boss, "Are you sure there's no more filing I can do for you?"
Anyone cheerful is an endangered species.	Anyone grouchy is a killjoy.

PART 8

Special Skills

How to Get the Most Out of Your Job

1. Change the meaning of working 9 to 5. Come in nine minutes before your boss does and leave five minutes later. Thus, if he's coming in tomorrow at noon, you need not be there until 11:51.
2. Use the elaborate phone system to connect your good friends in Albany with their relatives in Rome.
3. When ordering lunches for the board meeting, add a dozen side orders of chef salads, yogurt, and other lunch items the board doesn't like but their secretaries do.
4. In a memo from your boss to the company president, mention that she will be a few minutes late for her luncheon appointment due to a brief meeting with her secretary to discuss a much overdue salary increase.
5. Reroute the messenger through your favorite department store as a shortcut to his crosstown destination. Arm him with a large bill, and explain that the best place to get change for this COD delivery is at the cosmetic counter, where he only needs to make a small purchase.

A Dozen Creative New Things to Do with Wite-Out

1. Use as nail polish when you feel kinky.
2. Paint bull's eyes on your boss's glasses.
3. Write tiny obscene graffiti on office staplers.
4. Alter the family photos on the boss's desk.

5. Redirect the unwanted mail and office memos.
6. Use it to cover facial blemishes and blackheads.
7. Reletter typewriter keys for your own convenience.
8. Eliminate "unwanted" phone numbers from your boss's personal directory.
9. Fill the soap dispenser in the ladies' room.
10. Eliminate "undesirable" days from your boss's desk or wall calendar.
11. Remove the lipstick smear from your boss's collar following his three-hour-long "business lunch."
12. Suggest that your boss leave town long enough for her office to be repainted . . . with Wite-Out.

What to Say

Appropriate Secretarial Answers

The good secretary will always know what to say and when to say it. Here are a few examples of appropriate remarks to use in the office. The following examples are guaranteed to leave a definite impression upon your supervisors.

1. If your boss refers to herself as your superior, you should reply, "The only thing superior about you is your salary."
2. Should your supervisor say, "How about a cup of coffee?" you should respond, "Thank you, I take it with cream and two sugars."
3. After your boss has taken a cup of water from the watercooler, you should do the same and, before drinking, peer into your cup and exclaim "Look, a guppy!"
4. Should a demanding visitor grumble that he needs to see your boss in the worst way, you should suggest that he take a good look at her after one of her three-martini lunches.
5. Should your boss comment on your tardiness, saying that the early bird catches the worm, you should ask,

"Then why has no one caught you yet?"

6. If your boss should point out that it's five after nine, you should comment on the fact that she really should get that stupid watch repaired.

Calling In Sick, Late, or Dead

It's Monday morning, it's raining, your head still aches from Saturday night's party, and you haven't used a sick day in over two weeks. Today's the perfect opportunity for you to sleep late, catch up on your favorite soap opera, and dye your hair. First, however, you have to call in sick.

The actual call will take some preparation—perhaps even a short script. You must be poised, prepared, and precise. Any sense of doubt or guilt in your voice will give you away. You must also remember to avoid yawning, giggling or hiccupping.

First choose your illness or reason for taking the day off. If you just feel like coming in late and saving your sick days for sunshiny beach weather, any repairman you choose to wait for is on his way over. Calling in sick for a day requires a short-term illness such as a virus. A cold will require acting out symptoms for the next several days, and you may not have the time for a quick course in method acting.

Here are some appropriate lines for calling in sick, and what they really mean. Use them in good health!

1. *I won't be coming in today—my head is all stuffy and I think I'm coming down with something.*

In other words:
- The weekend party had longer-lasting effects than I thought.
- My head is full of illicit thoughts, and my lover is taking the day off with the same malady.
- I've got a severe case of Monday morning commuter blues and my allergies to mass transit are acting up.

2. *I won't be in today—I think I've got a twenty-four-hour bug and ache all over.*
   In other words:
   - I think the twenty-two rides on the Cyclone at Great Adventure Amusement Park are still affecting my equilibrium.
   - After eight hours in the sun I can barely move, much less lift my arms to type.
   - There's an incredible one-day-only sale that I wouldn't miss for the world.

3. *I can't come in today. I think I sprained my ankle and I'd better stay off it just in case.*
   In other words:
   - I'm spending the day in bed, with company.

- I'm spending the day in bed sleeping 'til noon, with two good books, three good soap operas, a host of Hostess junk food, and the Home Shopping Network.
- I did the Jane Fonda workout tape on fast forward and sprained everything!

And for those occasions that border on the unique, read on.

4. *I can't come in today—I've got some personal matters to attend to.*
   In other words:
   - I'm going to write my novel, learn to play the piano, eat an entire pizza, read an entire book.
   - I'm in the mood to join a religious cult group, or at least a health club.
   - I have an overwhelming urge to redecorate my apartment in a combination of American Indian and Los Angeles Punk.
   - I've got an appointment with a psychic to read my palm, tea leaves, and the last three issues of *TV Guide*.

The day after calling in "sick," you must be prepared to explain that you feel fine, and don't know exactly what was wrong yesterday, but it was the worst. If you can discuss your "illness" with a slightly nauseous expression and a whimper in your voice, it'll be more effective.

Deaths in the family are less effective for an adult than they were for you when you killed your grandfather off eight times as a child. The last thing you want is unwarranted sympathy cards. And if you do kill off a relative you'd better be prepared for ramifications, because there's one person in every office who loves to attend funerals and hear all the gory details.

Remember to leave your answering machine on at all times. You can always say you were asleep, and not let on that you were out living it up.

If you run out of every possible excuse and you're sick of psychological warfare—not to mention your job—then simply call in dead. Who can argue with that one?

Never Tell Your Boss . . .

1. That you found a coworker or two sleeping in her office when you came in at 8:30 A.M.

2. The real number of times you typed her letter.

3. Who spilled Wite-Out on her desk blotter.

4. That she has no taste in clothing.

5. What he really said to you after three glasses of punch at last year's Christmas party.

6. That you've been dating her son.

7. That she wears more make-up than Tammy Bakker.

8. The tone of her spouse's voice on the phone.

9. That you saw him leaving the Pussycat Burlesque.

10. That you saw the toilet paper stuck to her shoe as she walked into that meeting.

11. That you found the bottle of liquor in his bottom drawer.

12. That you drank some of that liquor from the bottle in her bottom drawer.

13. What you really think of his jokes.

14. That you discovered those "lost" reports under the plant by your desk.

15. That her son is a drag queen.

16. Who really backed into his left taillight in the parking lot.

17. That you posed nude in a magazine.

18. That it was you who overheard her story about a tryst with an out-of-town executive and started the gossip wheels in motion.

19. That you forgot to rinse the soap out of the coffeepot before making him his afternoon brew.

20. How many of her mistakes you really catch.

21. That your greatest fiction-writing achievement was your resume.

22. That the chicken you ordered up for his lunch was actually frog's legs.

23. That one of your two hours of overtime last night (after she left) was spent on a challenging crossword puzzle.

24. That you've been after his job and just got it!

25. That you use his prized golf trophy cup to water the plants.

Twenty Good Reasons Why Your Boss Can't Take His Calls

Sometimes it's hard to deal with persistent callers, especially when they've heard the same lame excuses a hundred times. So here's a new and improved list of things to say when your boss either can't or won't take a call. Simply grit your teeth and say, "I'm sorry, but . . ."

1. "Mr. Johnson is on a long-distance call—to another planet."
2. "Mr. Johnson is on a long-distance flight—would you care to hold until he lands?"
3. "Mr. Cornfeld's tied up at the moment—in black leather and chains."
4. "Mr. Page is on the other line with the President."
5. "Mr. Page is on the other line with the Pope."
6. "Mr. Page is on the other line with God!"
7. "Mr. Simmons can't come to the phone right now—he's practicing his putting in the reception area."
8. "Mr. Walker is sunbathing on the window ledge—please hold."
9. "Mr. Trivex is busy shredding his last six months' correspondence at the moment."
10. "Mr. Wexler is busy watching the afternoon soaps—please call back after four."
11. "Miss Franklin is beheading one of her staff—please hold."
12. "Mr. Palmer is busy with another call girl—I mean, Mr. Palmer is busy with another call, girl."
13. "Mr. Carstairs is trying to figure out how to work the pencil sharpener. Can you call back?"
14. "Miss Pimm has just tried to hang herself after reading the annual financial report."
15. "Mr. Nevins will be with you as soon as hell freezes over—can you hold?"
16. "Mr. Richards is busy cheating on his wife. Please call back."
17. "Ms. Lindsay is busy with clients who've just arrived from Mars."
18. "Mrs. Smith doesn't have her dentures in at the moment; you wouldn't be able to understand a word she said even if she did come to the phone."
19. "Mr. Wade says he'll get back to you the day the Pope gets bar mitzvahed.
20. "Mr. Marx can't speak to you or anyone else for that matter, since he's dead."

How to Stretch Your Lunch Hour

As we all know, a mere hour is never enough of a respite from the daily grind—or enough time to accomplish your many personal chores and errands, never mind eating lunch. If you can no longer get by with taking two or more hours for lunch without an explanation, here are some other handy ways to stretch your lunch hour:

1. Throw a party for a coworker, timed to begin when your lunch hour ends.
2. Shop madly for an hour, hide the clothes in the office ladies' room, and try them on at intervals during the afternoon.
3. Order in lunch not only for your boss, but for all the other executives and coworkers in your area. Always take detailed, individual orders and use several different coffee shops, delis, and pizzerias. The resulting confusion—sorting out orders, taking money, and giving change, etc.—will stretch out the time and also give you the opportunity of chatting with coworkers, sharing bits and pieces of their lunches, etc.
4. Schedule doctor and dentist appointments either right before or right after your lunch hour, and develop as many dental, periodontal and physical problems as you can think up.
5. Encourage your boss to let you handle his banking matters and as many personal chores, such as shopping for his relatives, as possible. If there is a wife *and* a mistress involved, this can double your "free time" and sometimes make your "lunch hour" last all day, especially during the holiday season.
6. When you have something special planned, such as a romantic lunch-hour reunion with an old boyfriend, hire an out-of-work female friend to act as your clone. Have her make herself up, dress in your clothes, and sit at your desk for the number of hours you plan to be gone. If you decide not to come back that day at all, you're covered—just make sure she's of your same race and that she can type and answer the phone.

Ten Easy Steps to a Three-and-a-Half-Hour Lunch

If you carefully follow these steps in order, you'll have plenty of time to stuff your face, buy a new outfit, go on a job interview, and even take in an afternoon movie.

1. At about 11:00 A.M., inconspicuously pour the remaining coffee down the sink.

2. Wait for numerous complaints that there is no more coffee, and volunteer to go out to buy some. Tell your boss that you'll be back in fifteen minutes. Take thirty and complain about the long lines. (Total lunch time: Half an hour.)

3. Tell only your boss that you're not going out for lunch today.

4. Have a cup of yogurt at your desk. (Total lunch time: one and a half hours.)

5. Act like you're working when anyone passes by. (Keep the magazine on your lap under your desk.)

6. When your boss goes for lunch, tell everyone else that it's also your lunch hour, and leave. (Total lunch time: Two and a half hours.)

7. Return before your boss does.

8. Complain that you're feeling dizzy, and hint that you're still hungry after having "just" a cup of yogurt.

9. When your boss finally suggests that perhaps you didn't eat enough for lunch, agree with her "intuitive" prognosis.

10. She'll give you a brief lecture on how a normal lunch is necessary to produce your best work, and you'll be on your way once again. (Total lunch time: Three and a half hours.)

Emergency Excuses Upon Returning Late from Lunch

You've probably used every excuse in the book by now—and exhausted your imagination as far as the subject of lunchtime lateness is concerned. So here are a few emergency excuses so bizarre and shocking they're guaranteed to stop your boss's tirade in its tracks and, hopefully, save your butt one more time . . .

1. There was a holdup at the bank—literally.

2. There was a holdup at the bank, and I couldn't decide who to take as a hostage.

3. I sprained my ankle and had to go to the hospital emergency room. (Be sure to stop at the drugstore and purchase an Ace bandage. Wrap it around your ankle and practice your limp on the way back to your office.)

4. My purse was snatched and I went to the police station. Then I spent an hour shopping for a new one, not to mention matching shoes.

5. The bus I was riding on was hijacked.
6. The restaurant I was eating in exploded.
7. My lunch date had a nervous breakdown and I had to escort her back to the clinic.
8. My ex-boss threatened suicide unless I went back to work for him. When I turned him down, in spite of the incredible salary he offered, he climbed out the window ledge and I had to help the police talk him out of jumping!

And if your boss believes the above excuses, you get the lunch-hour Academy Award. It's not an Oscar. It's an Oscar Mayer.

The After-Lunch Syndrome

Coping with Your Boss

Sometimes your boss may return from lunch a little worse for wear—or a lot worse. When this happens you will have to "cover for him," and at times this will be more complicated than just leading her to her couch and covering her with her coat while she sleeps it off. Depending upon your boss's occasional or habitual condition upon returning from lunch, you may be called upon to develop the following skills:

1. Propping her up at her desk.
2. The use of breath and room fresheners.
3. Ignoring propositions and passes.
4. Fielding her calls.
5. Failing that, the use of ventriloquism.
6. Forging her signature.
7. Brewing coffee strong enough to walk by itself.
8. Serving coffee with a funnel.
9. Cancelling important appointments.
10. Failing that, the use of emergency impersonation.
11. Bringing her to.
12. Knocking her out.
13. Getting her out of the office in a vertical position.
14. Convincing taxis to act as ambulances.
15. Filling your boss in on what actually happened, should she remember to ask the next day.
16. Learning to edit the horrific truth into a single innocuous sentence, such as: "Everything went smoothly."

Ten Fun Things to Do While Your Boss Is on Vacation

1. Take two lunch hours, yours and hers.

2. Use her office for a jewelry, lingerie, or Tupperware party.

3a. Put a small portable TV in your Out Box, and keep everyone abreast of the daily soap operas.

3b. Type up a newsletter to further update your coworkers on the soaps.

4. Use your boss's office for self-awareness classes.

5. Park your car in her designated parking space.

6. Closely "inspect" the personnel files.

7. Finish that novel you were reading and start writing one on the office computer.

8. Have friends and family spend the day with you.

9. Watch movies on the boss's VCR.

10. Stay home.

Meetings

How to Sleep Through Them with Your Eyes Open

The art of inconspicuously sleeping through a meeting is an ancient art developed by the Egyptians during pyramid architectural-planning sessions. To successfully remain wide-eyed and appear to be fully awake requires a degree of deep concentration similar to self-hypnosis.

First, you must relax and feel comfortable in your selected or assigned seat. It is a good idea to speak to several people just prior to the start of the meeting. This will enhance the belief that you are awake and alert.

To set the mood, picture the conference table as a small bar, with the office chairs as lounge chairs. Feel the air-conditioning as a cool tropical breeze, pretend your diet Sprite is a margarita, and imagine you're on the beach behind your hotel in Barbados. Your boss's voice is that of the bartender chatting with the other guests as they sit around the bar. Your only concern is that you don't get too much sun. The lighting above you is a clear sky without a cloud in it. Now you can quietly slip your shoes off and imagine the rug is the sand below your feet. You see a building through the window, a resort hotel farther down the beach. Now you are completely at peace with your surroundings, relaxed and dreaming. You don't have a single care in the world.

Suddenly you hear your name called and you see people looking at you. Your boss says, "Well?" and you quickly respond, "Another margarita, please."

Working 9 to 5, 9 to 4, 9 to 3 . . .

Shortening the Workday

Shortening the workday is a difficult task unless you've worked out a deal with Mother Nature to provide well-timed snowstorms or perhaps an impending hurricane. Although you're unable actually to control the weather, you may be able to alter your boss's perception of it if she has a VCR in the office. All you have to do is slip a tape of an old weather forecast, which includes any type of appropriate impending storm warning, into the VCR and let it play part of *The Morning News Report.*

You could always use the weather as an ally. By making sure that either the heat or the air-conditioning isn't working, you could shorten your workday. Forgetting to pay the heating bill for three months may create a cool atmosphere. But using blue ink from the stamp pad on your lips while chattering your teeth might convince your boss that it's far too cold to keep the office open. In the summer you might choose to "accidentally" jam the switch on the air-conditioner. If you then work up a sweat by running up and down the stairs once or twice, you might have her convinced that it's just too hot to continue.

In larger offices you'll need the cooperation of your coworkers or perhaps another plan, such as a blackout, or a paint out. Neglecting to pay the electric bill for six months is the easiest way to create a blackout. A paint out is where the office painters are creating such havoc that it's simply impossible to keep working. To accomplish this, simply find non-English-speaking painters and have them work with colors they've never used before. Make sure they cover everything over, and keep getting in their way. Eventually they'll convey the message to your boss that they just can't work in this manner.

How to Tell If Your Boss Is a Bad Guy

There are good bosses, there are bad bosses, and then there are *bad* bosses. These are those rare few who really can't be trusted. Fortunately, most secretaries catch on quickly to a dangerous boss, but just in case you're not sure, here is a short list of ways to tell if you're working for a rat.

You know your boss is up to no good when:

1. He asks you to work on Saturday, and you find only you and your boss are in the office. Then your boss confronts you carrying a bottle of champagne and suggests celebrating annual report week.
2. He sends you to the bank, in Switzerland.
3. She informs you that your raise depends on how much she likes what you give her for Christmas.
4. He starts ducking phone calls from two guys named Vinnie and Rocco.
5. His five children show up, with five different mothers.
6. Something in his Out Box is ticking.
7. She starts asking you to smuggle out files under your clothing.
8. He tries to assist you in placing those files under your clothing.
9. She tells you to accept calls from the KGB.
10. He installs a back door behind the bookshelves in his office.

Where's the Boss?

Should You Really Say?

An efficient secretary should always be able to locate his boss in the event that there is an important business matter requiring immediate attention, or lunch is getting cold.

Try to acquaint yourself with your boss's daily and weekly routine. It is helpful if you know when and where he usually does his banking, his shopping, his drinking, etc. Get to know his contacts. Find out the names of his barber, his dentist, his bookie, his mistress, and the rest of his favorite foursome on the golf course.

If you're able to track him down at any given time, you'll either be of vital importance or a colossal pain in the neck. Your success might prompt you to consider a career as a detective.

You must, however, remember that your boss enjoys and appreciates privacy, and should only be contacted for reasons of the utmost importance, such as: your company declaring bankruptcy; a fire in the office; an irate but important client throwing a fit in the outer office; a pregnant woman urgently wanting to see him; or his winning the company football pool.

Most important, you must be tactful if you're in the process of dragging your boss away from a poker game while he's holding three kings. Present any such matter as a major emergency that only he could possibly solve—and remember, anything less and you'll never be trusted again. Few people realize that two of Henry the Eighth's wives (whom he had beheaded) were also his secretaries and that their only crimes were interrupting his afternoon tea. Therefore, it's important to be able to track down your boss, but think twice, or even thrice, about actually doing so.

How to Kill Your Boss—Quietly

1. Accidentally bump into your boss while carrying his gold letter opener.
2. Instead of using a dairy product, use Wite-Out in her coffee.
3. Show him the new, hip way of tying a necktie so that the blue in his face matches the blue in his shirt.
4. If he's over sixty-five, send him a Strip-o-Gram.
5. Hold the elevator door open for her on the fifth floor while the elevator is still on the second floor.

PART 9

After Hours

Sex and the Single Secretary

If you're dating someone with wonderful fingers and the uncanny ability to put any conversation on hold, then you're probably dating a secretary. Secretaries may proofread your love notes, but they can also read between the lines. Since part of a secretary's job is discerning good visitors from bad ones, and sincere callers from phonies, secretaries are quite proficient at reading people. If you hand a secretary a line, she'll file it, type it, edit it, copy it, mail it, or put it on a yellow pad of paper and stick it to the wall, but she won't fall for it (at least not unless she wants to).

Sexually, secretaries have fast fingers and a gentle touch, which comes from touch typing. Administrative secretaries enjoy a "top" position, while personal secretaries enjoy catering to your needs and desires.

Whereas there's always hot coffee brewing the following morning, the one drawback to fooling around with a secretary is that she habitually answers all phone calls, which can be distracting during sex. You should also try to discourage your secretarial lover from bringing a rubber finger into the bedroom—unless you want to get kinky.

All in all, the consensus is that secretaries make good partners. Most have experience working with a "Wang" and know what to do with "software." And since they do a great deal of filing, one might say that secretaries enjoy sexuality from A to Z.

The Secretary's Hit Parade

"Working 9 to 5"
"Take This Job and Shove It"

"Fingertips" (An ode to touch typing)
"16 Tons" (What the mail at Xmas feels like)
"You're Gonna Lose That Gal" (Friday)
"I Could Have Danced All Night"
"Hold On, I'm Coming" (Back from lunch)
"Everybody's Talking At Me"
"Never on a Sunday" (An ode to overtime)
"You Give Work a Bad Name"
"Ain't No Mountain (of papers) High Enough"
"The Great Pretender" (A tribute to resumes)
"Born to Lose" (Messages)
"Can't Steno Without You"
"I've Just Gotta Take a Message from You"
"Tie A Typing Ribbon 'Round the Old Boss's Neck"
"Talk to the Animals" (An ode to visitors)
"All She Wants to Do Is Type"
"Turn, Turn, Turn" (An ode to a Rolodex)
"So Many Jobs, So Little Time"
"Ricky, Don't Lose That Number"
"Moonlighting Serenade"
"And Take a Message to Michael"
"Just Another Manic Monday"

The Secretary's Favorite Films

★★★★★★★★★★★★★★★★★★

ROBOSEC'Y

★★★★★★★★★★★★★★★★★★

Mechanized secretarial robot runs amok when she develops a crush on her boss and becomes insanely jealous of her gum-chewing, big-busted counterparts. Coffee breaks turn into bloodbaths—not for those with weak stomachs or high IQs.

★★★★★★★★★★★★★★★★★★

HANNAH AND HER BLISTERS

★★★★★★★★★★★★★★★★★★

The haunting story of a Coney Island secretary in the 1930s who works for a radio station and is forced to use carbon paper and type on a manual until her fingers turn blue and blistered.

★★★★★★★★★★★★★★★★★★

WASTEBASKET CASE

★★★★★★★★★★★★★★★★★★

The chilling story of a secretary and her evil, trash-eating mini-twin who eventually feels slighted and begins eating the other secretaries' eye makeup, *Cosmo* mags, and refrigerated luncheon salads!

★★★★★★★★★★★★★★★★★★

HIGH NOON

★★★★★★★★★★★★★★★★★★

A young, blond secretary and her older, tight-assed boss have a showdown over her lunch hour at their office in a sleepy western town.

★★★★★★★★★★★★★★★★★★

ROSEMARY'S APPLE

★★★★★★★★★★★★★★★★★★

A successful Manhattan secretary is mysteriously molested by her company's high-tech equipment, develops a craving for raw pastrami, and gives birth to an embarrassingly prosaic personal computer!

★★★★★★★★★★★★★★★★★★
NINE TO FIVE, III
★★★★★★★★★★★★★★★★★★

Who put the arsenic in the office coffee maker and installed a mini-guillotine in the men's room stalls? The three increasingly psychotic secretaries, of course!

★★★★★★★★★★★★★★★★★★
THE TEXAS CHAIN LETTER MASSACRE
★★★★★★★★★★★★★★★★★★

Slow-witted Waco teenagers are terrorized by threatening chain letters printed in blood-red ink and mailed out from the local sausage link factory by spinster secretary Aieda De Pork.

★★★★★★★★★★★★★★★★★★
MY FAIR CLEANING LADY
★★★★★★★★★★★★★★★★★★

A rollicking, heartwarming musical about an eccentric boss who's determined to turn the illiterate female immigrant who cleans the office after hours into an executive secretary with a perfect command of typing, shorthand, and the English language.

★★★★★★★★★★★★★★★★★★
THE PHANTOM OF THE OFFICE
★★★★★★★★★★★★★★★★★★

Supernatural thriller about a cruelly demanding, deceased French boss who comes back to haunt the American Express office in Paris, forcing innocent, modern-day secretaries to do office work that has been overdue since the 1890s.

★★★★★★★★★★★★★★★★★★
FATAL DISTRACTION
★★★★★★★★★★★★★★★★★★

Hot-blooded young secretary becomes so involved in having sex with her boss on his desk that she doesn't notice his wife has entered the room with a video camera, causing major embarrassment to all three of them.

Secretaries' Answering Machine Messages

"Hi, this is Joyce. I'm sorry I'm not home right now, but I'm never home, because I'm always at work. I'd give you my work number, except that I'm not allowed to receive personal calls."

"Hello, Mr. Smithers isn't in right now. How could he be, since this is my phone? But if you leave your name, your company's name, your phone number, your extension, your secretary's name, as well as a brief description of what this is in reference to, either Mr. Smithers or I will get back to you as soon as he calls my answering machine or I call his."

"Hi, this is Elaine. I can't come to the phone right now, since I'm getting some much-needed sleep, but you can leave a message at the sound of the tone.

Yes, Mr. Smithers, this applies to you too. Not even the devil himself could get me up right now!"

"You have reached 747-7744. Please feel free to leave your name and number at the sound of the beep. If I had a secretary I would have her get back to you, but being a secretary myself, I don't have the strength . . ."

"This is Theresa. I can't come to the phone right now, so if you want to leave a message please make it short and sweet and to the point, because I left all my shorthand at the office, along with my sweetness—get the point?"

"Hi, this is Sally. If you leave your name and number at the sound of the beep I probably won't get back to you, since it'll remind me too much of work, so if you have any romantic interest at all, you'd better think up some clever, spontaneous way of meeting up with me in person!"

My Mom, the Secretary

Here's what some youngsters have had to say about their secretary-moms:

1. She doesn't tie my shoes, she staples them."
   —Stacy, age seven
2. "She always hides my birthday presents in her desk."
   —Nathan, age six
3. "My mom can type faster than I can read!"
   —Terry, age 10
4. "Mommy takes letters—I think she is a postman."
   —Lisa, age three
5. "I have the best-typed book reports in class!"
   —Evan, age 11
6. "She has me sign for my allowance, then makes me fill out an expense report."
   —Joseph, age 13
7. "Mommy takes her boss's dictation . . . is that like taking my temperature?"
   —Rachel, age five
8. "Mommy says looking after her boss is just like taking care of me, only worse."
   —Dennis, age four

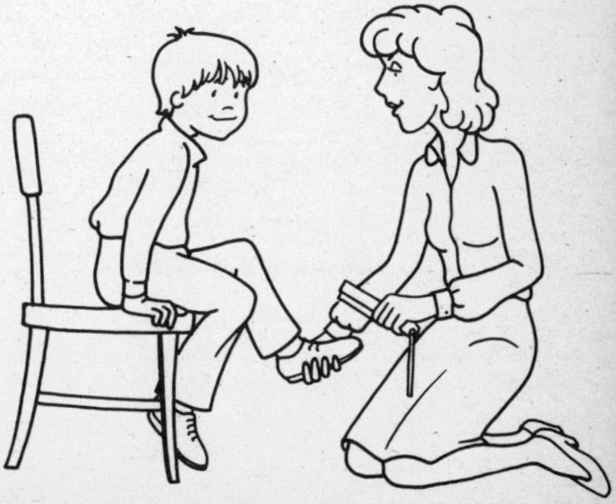

PART 10

Quitting Time

IS YOUR BOSS INSANE?
A Quickie Quiz

1. **When your boss is in a really bad mood, you have to hide the:**
   (A) Overdue bills.
   (B) Nasty letters and messages.
   (C) Letter opener.

2. **The last time you went on vacation, your boss:**
   (A) Replaced you with a temp.
   (B) Called you constantly.
   (C) Sat motionless for a week.

3. **When your boss doesn't care for food you ordered, she:**
   (A) Sends it back.
   (B) Throws it away.
   (C) Eats it only to have the pleasure of complaining about it for the rest of the day.

4. **The last time the air-conditioning broke down, your boss asked you to:**
   (A) Call maintenance.
   (B) Call in a fan dancer.
   (C) Take your clothes off.

5. **Your boss wishes you'd be more like the following TV personality:**
   (A) Loni Anderson.
   (B) Mary Tyler Moore.
   (C) Pee Wee Herman.

6. On your last birthday, your boss sent you:
(A) Flowers.
(B) A male stripper.
(C) To the bargain basement to pick out your own gift.

7. When asked what kind of plant he wanted in his office, your boss replied:
(A) A wandering Jew.
(B) A Venus fly trap.
(C) A female Russian spy.

8. If you find your boss standing on the outside window ledge, it would be because:
(A) There was a fire.
(B) The stock market crashed again.
(C) He was flashing again.

9. When your boss gets really upset, the best way to calm her down is by giving her:
(A) A shot of booze.
(B) A shot upside the head.
(C) A shot of animal tranquilizer administered with a dart gun.

10. If you misspelled a word in a letter, your boss would:
(A) Call you on not looking it up.
(B) Call you an idiot.
(C) Call your fifth grade teacher and demand an apology for failing to teach you how to spell.

How to Know When It's Time to Leave Your Job

Often the toughest decision you'll face in the office is when it's time to leave—for good. In most offices, five o'clock ends the workday, and Friday ends the workweek. But when does the job itself come to an end?

In the event that your fate has been decided by your higher-ups, you are spared the decision-making problem. Leaving your job in this manner can be difficult if it does not give your co-workers sufficient time to plan a farewell party and buy a card for everyone to sign. Being dismissed generally requires that you vacate the premises somewhat abruptly, leaving you little or no time to totally screw up the files, and pollute the watercooler. In this situation, however, you'll have plenty of time to plan and plot your revenge while waiting on the unemployment lines.

If it is your decision to leave, you should give your boss two weeks' notice before you disappear. There are bosses, companies, and jobs, however, that simply aren't worthy of such common courtesy. In these circumstances you might choose to leave for lunch and never return. Another tactful way to leave your job is to take a paid leave of absence for the rest of your life. If your company gives unlimited sick days, you might start taking them—and continue to phone in sick each morning from your new job—until they figure that your physical health is not the real issue.

There are usually surefire signs screaming out that it is time to call it quits. Should you begin looking at help-wanted signs in McDonald's windows with a slight degree of interest, or feel a sense of guilt over not working in your uncle's macaroni strainer factory, then you may be ready to leave your job.

Below is a checklist of other signs that may be telling you it's time to move on.

You know it's time to leave your job when:

1. You are specifically asked not to attend a meeting.
2. You see the job applicants scouting out your cubicle.
3. Tellers giggle as you cash your paycheck.
4. You start enjoying the music in the elevators so much that you don't want to get off at your floor.
5. The envelope with your Christmas bonus in it jingles.
6. You kick the copy machine and could swear it kicked you back.
7. Everyone but you is taught how to use the new computer system.
8. You start finding the job section from the Sunday paper on your desk Monday morning.
9. Friends you thought would never amount to anything are earning twice as much as you.
10. You consider the possibility of opening up a hot dog stand as a lateral move in the right direction.

Twenty Ways to Leave Your Employer

Here are a few tips on how to quit, or get yourself fired from your current position:

1. Take an endless lunch hour.
2. Join the army.
3. Tell your boss you're moving to a friendlier place behind the Iron Curtain.

4. Eat until you explode.
5. Refuse to shower or bathe for two weeks.
6. Wear your "Take This Job and Shove It" T-shirt to a meeting with your supervisors.
7. Tell your boss you'd like to do a thesis on the workings of the unemployment insurance system.
8. Practice your karate on your coworkers.
9. Prepare a new recipe for Fire-Alarm Chili and force-feed it to your boss.
10. Refuse to fit into the Plumbing Company's "image."
11. Slip your resignation into a fortune cookie when your boss orders Chinese food.
12. Get into a heated dispute with your coworkers over which restaurant to order lunch from, and storm out of the office exclaiming, "I quit!"
13. Insist upon bringing your cat to work with you.
14. Plan your boss's travel itinerary, and then go in her place.

15. Send your boss a cake with the words "I'm Out Of Here" written on it.

16. Join a South American revolutionary organization.

17. Slowly, over a period of days, inch your desk and chair into the elevator, and press DOWN.

18. Throw a rock into your boss's window with a properly typed, polite resignation letter attached to it.

19. Ask your boss for a raise in person at her home at 3 A.M.

20. Get coffee for your boss—in Brazil.

PART 11

Secretarial Humor

From the Joke File

JANET: My boss is upset because when I was out sick he had to type his own letter and it took him an hour and a half.

CINDY: To type the letter?

JANET: No, to figure out how to turn the typewriter on.

Then there was the girl who only went to work at the end of the week. It seemed she took the title Gal Friday literally.

My secretary, Bob, makes up for all my errors. In fact, now he's living with my ex-wife.

One secretary recounted the problem with dating a personnel director. To break up with him she had to give him two weeks' notice!

As they drove to work, the male secretary, Jay, turned to the female secretary, Dee, and said, "Look, there's our boss, Mrs. Kaye—should we pick her up? There's room between us."

"No," replied Dee, "last time I put K between J and D she nearly fired me."

Then there was the secretary who set up bowling pins on the office floor. It seems she heard that the company was doing poorly and heads were about to roll.

"Even as a child I was shy," explained the secretary. "My friends would play doctor. One would be the doctor, one the nurse, and one the patient. I was always the patient's secretary, who simply had to call ahead to make sure the appointment was confirmed."

The secretary turned around from the new Xerox machine and was startled at the sight of her boss opening his pants. "Mr. Wilson," she gasped, "the machine only enlarges paper!"

As the boss and a prostitute looked up from under the desk at the woman in the doorway, the secretary poked her head in and said, "I thought perhaps your wife would help me ask you for that long overdue raise you've been promising me."

"Are you sure she can't see me yet?" asked the impatient young man. "She'll let me know when she's ready for you to see her," replied the secretary.

"Yeah, I know," he responded anxiously, "but it's our honeymoon!"

In the middle of typing a letter, the secretary turned off the Dictaphone, went into her boss's office, and said, "I went through half of your letter, but I got stuck. I'm just not sure how to indicate snoring."

"My boss was always bitching about his swimming pool, so I put a shark in it," quipped the secretary. "This way when he says it costs an arm and a leg to maintain it, I'll believe him!"

"We've got a great new talking scale in our office for everyone who's on a diet," explained the secretary to her friend.

"Isn't that embarrassing?" asked her friend.

"Not really," responded the secretary. "I progammed it the same way my boss trained me . . . to lie a lot."

The entire office could hear the secretary on the phone yelling at the supply department: "Wheels on my desk? I didn't say roller desk, I said Rolodex!"

"This is the muddiest coffee you've ever made," shouted the nearsighted senior V.P.

"Here are your glasses, Mr. Sloan," replied the secretary, "and you're drinking your desk plant."

Bartlett's Secretary's Quotations

"To be or not to be a secretary . . . that is the question."

* * *

"Oh secretary, my secretary, wherefore art thou secretary!"

* * *

"Four score and seven secretaries ago, our fathers brought forth a new company . . ."

* * *

"Ask not what your secretary can do for you, but what you can do for your secretary."

* * *

"Frankly, my dear secretary, I don't give a damn."

* * *

"My secretary likes a red, red rose."

* * *

"Hell hath no fury like a secretary scorned!"

* * *

"Behind every great man there's a secretary."

* * *

"Behind every secretary there's a boss . . . hiding."

* * *

"When the boss is away, the secretaries will play."

* * *

"What do secretaries really want?"